AF601574

Foreword by Congressman Emanuel Cleaver, II

A MAN MADE OF STEEL

A TRIBUTE TO MY FATHER AND OTHER GREAT AFRICAN AMERICAN FATHERS

DR. RODNEY D. SMITH

A MAN MADE OF STEEL

A TRIBUTE TO MY FATHER AND OTHER GREAT AFRICAN AMERICAN FATHERS

DR. RODNEY D. SMITH

SOPHIC SOLUTIONS
KANSAS CITY, MO

A Man Made of Steel
Written by Dr. Rodney D. Smith
Book Design by Cynthia L. Robinson
Author Headshot by Kenney Ellison Photography

Sophic Solutions
Kansas City, MO
rodney@sophicsolutionsgroup.com
sophicsolutionsgroup.com

Ordering Information:
Quantity sales. Special discounts are available on quantity purchases by corporations, associations, and others. For details, contact the publisher at the email address above. Orders by U.S. trade bookstores and wholesalers.

Library of Congress Control Number: 2026907576

ISBN: 978-0-997-5241-4-7 (Hardcover)
ISBN: 978-0-997-5241-2-3 (Paperback)
ISBN: 978-0-997-5241-3-0 (ebook)

Printed in the
United States of America
First Edition

To great fathers

CONTENTS

FOREWORD

There are stories we inherit, and there are stories we must disrupt. For far too long, the story of the Black father has been told by those who neither know us fully nor love us wholly. This narrative has been controlled and manipulated by systems that benefit from our absence and are perpetuated by institutions that profit from our pain. What the world believes it knows about Black men, and especially Black fathers, is not true. We are engaged in a battle over narratives, and this book stands as part of our strategy to reclaim our story.

The myth of the malevolent Black man is not new. It is a centuries-old fabrication that originated during the times of conquest and colonization, was solidified during America's darkest chapters, and later ingrained into the structures of segregation and separation. Today, this lie has adopted new forms, it wears suits and ties, it communicates through policy language and technical jargon and hides behind seemingly neutral data. Yet, at its core, it remains the same lie. Its impact is devastating, costing us our dignity, our children, our future, and our nation.

My understanding of these truths does not come from books alone, it has also been shaped by my two decades of experience as the U.S. Representative for Missouri's 5th District. Every day, I am present at decision-making tables that determine the life outcomes of people, many of whom look like me. I work with individuals—some well-meaning, some indifferent—who hold power over communities they do not truly know. Through this work, I have learned that being close to power does not always mean being close to truth. I have also learned that politics is not a game, the stakes are high, and the consequences are profoundly impactful on the lives of the people we serve.

This is partly why I am encouraging you to read this book. This book tells the truth about a group of people I am well acquainted with—Black Fathers. This book was born out of the need to bridge the gap between the lived experiences of Black fathers and the distorted perceptions held by society. This book is both a lamentation and a proclamation, a song of resistance and a revelation of truth. This book is not a plea for permission to be seen, it is rather a demand for acknowledgment. The truth is clear, Black fathers are present. We are providers, protectors, pillars of perseverance, architects of resilience, and stewards of generational strength. We are not perfect, but we are powerful. We are here, and we have always been here.

This book is not only about the journey of fatherhood but also about its legacy. It explores what it means to raise children in a world that questions their worth before learning their names. It speaks to the quiet courage required to show up day after day in a society that often refuses to recognize your existence. It honors the sacred mission of loving your children while working to dismantle the falsehoods told about you and them.

This book also celebrates the joys and pleasures of fatherhood. It finds meaning in witnessing our children excel academically, in extracurricular activities, and, most importantly, in their growth as kind and responsible human beings. It is the pride of knowing that we have contributed to raising children who not only understand what is right, but who are committed to doing what is right. It is the satisfaction of knowing that you played a vital role in shaping productive lives.

At its core, this book is about telling the truth. Truth-telling is not only a moral obligation, but also a strategy for survival. When the world insists on defining you by your supposed deficiencies, telling your own story becomes an act of resistance. And when your story is rooted in love, truth, faith, and resilience, it becomes a powerful blueprint for liberation.

To all readers, this book will challenge your assumptions. It will ask you to let go of preconceived notions about Black fatherhood. It invites you to listen with humility and to see with a fresh perspective. Whether you are a father, son, daughter, policymaker, or simply someone who cares about justice, this book is for you. It serves as both a mirror and a map.

To my brothers and fellow fathers, this book is a love letter to you. It is a reminder that you are not alone, that your work matters, that your presence has power, and that your story is sacred. Regardless of what the world may say, there is nothing inherently wrong with you, and you are enough. This book honors you. You have shown, and continue to show, that true strength is not just physical, that love does not always need to be loud to be real, and that legacy is not just what you leave behind, but what you actively and intentionally build today. Rest assured, the values that you instill today will indeed carry into the future.

To the children and future generations who read this book, it is a promise to you. It declares that we, your fathers, will continue to fight to create a world that sees you clearly, loves you deeply, and never questions your worth. Let this book be your reckoning, your restoration, and a reminder that your existence is not a mistake and your father's love is not a flaw to be corrected, but an inheritance to be cherished.

Fatherhood is a blessing and a sacred calling. It is a reflection of the divine. It is a glimpse into the ways of God. "Fatherhood is arguably the closest mortal man comes to Godliness."[1] In light of this truth, let us not be disheartened by the manufactured lies and untruths that are told about us. Instead, let us stand steadfastly in our faith and be renewed, daily:

> *"[16]Therefore, we do not lose heart.... we are being renewed day by day. [17]For our light and momentary troubles are achieving for us an eternal glory that far outweighs them all. [18]So, we fix our eyes not on what is seen, but on what is unseen, since what is seen is temporary, but what is unseen is eternal."*[2]

Congressman Emanuel Cleaver, II
U.S. Representative for Missouri's 5th Congressional District

"If you have ever taken as truth any of the lies told about Black fathers, at the conclusion of this book, hopefully your beliefs will change."

A LETTER TO MY DAD

Dad,

As I have been writing this book, I have found myself returning to one truth over and over again, I have been blessed to have a father like you in my life. I have also discovered, over and over again, that I have been surrounded by several great fathers throughout my life. So in that respect, this book is not just mine. It belongs to us. It belongs to the men who have shown up, stood firm, and carried their families with a quiet strength the world too often refuses to see. And at the center of that truth, at the center of my life, is you.

I have always taken my responsibilities as a father seriously, and that is because I had a remarkable example to follow. I didn't have to imagine what an engaged, loving, steady father looked like. I lived with one. I was raised by one. I was shaped by one. You have been my most constant and powerful model of what fatherhood should be.

You have been the epitome of fatherhood, not just to me and Eric, but to so many others who found guidance, protection, and love in you. Some were family by blood, others by bond, but you never made a distinction. You fathered all of us with the same unwavering commitment.

In many ways, your years of work in the steel mill was more than a job. It served as a metaphor for the life you lived and the lives you helped to make better. You didn't just help make steel; you made strong people. You made men and women. You made a family that knows who it is because you showed us who you were.

You have been our anchor and example; the one we could always count on. In truth, you've been more than a hero. You've been our superhero.

This book is anchored in your presence because my life has been anchored in your presence. Every chapter, every insight, every challenge to the myths about Black fatherhood is rooted in the reality I witnessed growing up; a father who was always there.

Thank you for being the man who shaped me. Thank you for the steel you put in my spine and the love you put in my heart. Thank you for being my father, in every sense of the word.

With all my love and gratitude,

Rodney

INTRODUCTION

"Fiction becomes fact when it's the only version we see."
From a once known hand

I still remember the day Phoenix was born as if it were yesterday. She is our firstborn child. In fact, I remember the birth of all three of our children. Sadly, we lost our second child, Jordan, to a pre-term birth. At only 22 weeks, her little lungs had not developed enough to sustain her breathing. We were able to spend about 3 hours with her before she completed her earthly journey. Our son, Chi, completes the trio of our children. Fatherhood is one of the sweetest gifts God has ever given me.

While the trauma of losing Jordan has never left me, the birth of Phoenix, our first child, left an unforgettable mark too. In fact, my son's birth stands out as well. Because of our loss of Jordan, we had to take special measures to ensure his survival. In spite of these measures, we still had major complications related to his arrival. He actually arrived about a month early and needed some help breathing for the first few days of his life. He had to spend twelve days in the Neonatal Intensive Care Unit (NICU).

Despite these obstacles, the birth of Phoenix still stands out in my memory. Believe it or not, there were a host of people in the delivery room. My wife, though we were not officially married yet, had invited a number of her sorority sisters and friends to be a part of this wonderful day. My soon-to-be-mother-in-law was in the room as well. It was an exciting day to say the least.

My wife's friends were taking pictures and recording video clips of the whole experience. There was a buzz of excitement in the room. It was palpable. Perhaps the most accurate word to describe the feeling in the room is celebratory. The room was joyfully celebratory. It was euphoric.

Interestingly, the delivery physician and I were the only men in the room. He was the obstetrician on duty that day and was actually substituting for our regular obstetrician. As my daughter began to make her entrance, the physician began to give me insights on what to expect and offered instructions on how to cut the umbilical cord when the time came. However, what happened next, seemingly out of nowhere, drastically shifted the energy in the room. The energy eventually got back to where it was before the incident, but it definitely zapped a bit of the energy for at least a minute or two. It definitely affected my energy.

Among the people in the room, there were two or three nurses on hand to assist with the delivery. They were all busy doing their tasks in preparation for my daughter's arrival. And suddenly, one of the nurses, unprompted by anyone in the room, turned to me and asked, "who are you?" I replied, "I am the baby's father." She then turned to my fiancé, who was extremely preoccupied giving birth to our child at that moment and asked, "Do you want him in here?" My fiancé replied, "he's my baby's father, of course I want him in here."

Aside from being embarrassed by the situation, there were a million questions running through my mind. "Why did she just ask that?" "What made her believe that I did not deserve to be in the room?" How many times has she done this?" "If she's done this before, what were the reactions of the other fathers?" "Were they all African American fathers?" "What kind of relationship does she have with her father?" "Is she a mother, herself?" "If so, what kind of relationship does she have with her child/children's father?"

While I fully understand that mothers reserve the right to determine who is present in the delivery room, the nurse's questions caught me completely off guard. And to boot, she asked them with such vitriol, I could almost feel her words. It was as if she believed that she knew me or at least that she knew something about me. Even though she attempted to give some faint-hearted excuse about having seen estranged fathers forced their way into the delivery room, I resented her for a very long time for almost ruining one of the most important moments of my life. I had actually managed to stuff that memory away deep into the crevices of mind until recently. In preparation for this book, I read a variety of research articles, books and essays about Black fatherhood. One of those essays triggered this memory.

The birth of a first child is often described as a spiritual awakening, a moment when a person's identity begins to shift and deepen in many ways. It is a sacred moment. But unfortunately for me, this unforgettable moment of transformation was marred by a nurse's predetermined assumptions. Her questions, “Who are you?” and “Do you want him in here?” were much more than innocent requests for information, they were an intrusion into a moment that should have been entirely beautiful. Her questions carried the potential to completely shatter a very special moment. They also carried a poisonous venom that has long contaminated our country.

Her tone and timing were filled with prejudice and bias. Her questions reflected broader societal myths about Black men and Black Fatherhood. It exposed the widespread, yet false narratives that Black men are obstinate, that Black fathers are absent and disengaged, that we are “deadbeats.” Also, her questions assumed that Black children are all born into tumultuous circumstances. The fact that the moment still has a kind of psychological hold on me nearly twenty-five years later, lets you know how impactful the moment was.

Again, this sacred moment, the birth of a first child along with the cutting of the umbilical cord, an occasion that is widely understood as a rite of passage, was nearly ruined by a nurse’s flawed assumptions. Her questions were in many ways an attempt to sever, not the umbilical cord, but my rightful presence in the room and my undeniable identity as father. Take it as fact, the nurse’s questions were not simply an isolated incident. Her questions were reflective of widespread systemic views, opinions and misconceptions.

In America’s imagination, very few misnomers have been as stubbornly persistent and as damaging as those surrounding Black fatherhood and the Black family. These misnomers, born of systemic racism and perpetuated through media, public policy, and cultural narratives, have painted a distorted picture, one of absenteeism, dysfunction, and deficiency. But beneath these myths lies a deeper truth, one of presence, perseverance, and profound love.

Undoubtedly, the most pervasive misnomer is the idea that Black fathers are overwhelmingly absent from our children's lives. This narrative has been weaponized to suggest moral failure, cultural inadequacy, and a lack of responsibility. Yet data consistently reveals a more nuanced reality. Studies have shown that Black fathers, whether living with their children or not, are more involved in their children's lives than fathers from other racial groups.[1] The myth of absenteeism ignores the complexity of family structures and the resilience required to remain cohesive under the economic, social, and legal pressures that disproportionately affect Black families.

To understand the roots of these lies, we must confront the historical forces that have created them and thus have attempted to fracture Black families. From slavery, which tried to deny the very humanity of Black folk, to Jim Crow laws, mass incarceration, and discriminatory welfare policies, the Black family has been under siege. These systems did not simply damage family structure, they actively eroded them. And yet, despite these assaults, Black families have endured. We have adapted, redefined, and reimagined what family means, often expanding the concept to include extended kinfolk and community members—our chosen family.

Popular media, too, has played a central role in reinforcing these lies. Television, film, and news outlets often portray Black fathers as absent, irresponsible, and criminal.[2] Rarely do they show the quiet heroism of the Black father who works multiple jobs, who braids his daughter's hair *or at least tries to*, who teaches his son how to tie a tie, and how to not just survive, but how to thrive. These stories actually exist in abundance, but they are rarely told. The result is a cultural lens that sees pathology where there is, in reality, healthy family.

To dismantle these myths, we must reconstruct the narrative. This begins with listening to the voices of Black fathers and families. It means amplifying stories of love, sacrifice, and leadership. It means honoring the metaphysical heirlooms passed down through generations, the wisdom, prayers, and resilience of fathers. It means recognizing that Black fatherhood is not a deficit, but rather an asset to the entire country.

The misnomers of Black fatherhood are not just inaccurate, they are harmful. They shape and influence public perception and affect the self-image of Black children and parents alike. But truth has a way of breaking through. Every image, every article, every publication that honors the fullness of Black fatherhood is a step toward healing. It is a declaration that Black fatherhood is not invisible or absent. It is radiant as well as revelatory, but most importantly, it is real.

This book is unequivocally dedicated to Black Fatherhood. It is dedicated to the everyday, all-day, full-time, hands-on father. It is also dedicated to the dads who live apart from their children but do all they can, and more, to maintain an active presence in their children's lives. This book is dedicated to the fathers who do the daily and ordinary duties of fatherhood extraordinarily well. It is also dedicated to the fathers who have not always gotten it right but have vowed to right those wrongs.

This book is dedicated to us. I say us because I am one of those Black fathers. I take my responsibilities as a father very seriously. The beauty of my story is the fact that I have had a wonderful example to emulate. In fact, I have had multiple examples of great and engaged fathers to emulate. But my most prominent example has been by my side every step of my life's journey. He is my father, Mr. Zeddie C. Smith. I specifically and intentionally anchor the book around the ubiquitous presence and fatherly accomplishments of my dad.

He has been the epitome of fatherhood. He is the very definition of fatherhood. He has been the consummate father, not just to me and my brother, but to a host of other people, some biologically related and some not. He is a retired steelworker and has, literally and metaphorically, been making steel in two parallel ways. He has played a major part in producing some really strong and productive people. Again, he has fathered my entire family as well as a host of my friends. He has simply been "that dude" in our lives. He has been, not just our hero, but our superhero!

There are times, even today, that I will receive a phone call from a friend that I haven't seen or heard from in a while, and the exchange goes something like this, "Hey, I'm reaching out because I've lost your dad's contact information. Can I have his number? I need to talk to him about something." Often, on my weekly phone calls with my dad, *you read that correctly; I still speak with my dad on a weekly basis*, he will tell me about conversations and connections that he maintains with my friends, many of whom he has been a primary father-figure throughout their lives. Over the years, he has maintained a really active presence in my hometown, Georgetown, South Carolina. Again, he has been an important part of a lot of people's lives in my hometown.

Recently, he has curtailed his outreach and engagement a bit; I think largely because he is in his mid-80s now and likely does not have as much energy as he once did. But his energy and outreach still far exceeds that of individuals half his age. My father's legacy is and will be defined by his unwavering presence in our lives. He took the time to be there for us, to listen, and to guide us. This is a stark contrast to the flawed narratives about African American fathers.[3] My father defies these stereotypes, standing as a testament to the power of love, commitment, and presence. As the title of this book suggests, he is truly "A Man Made of Steel."

Like my dad, there are tons of African American men who maintain an active role in their children's lives. A few of them you will meet in the upcoming chapters. I have anchored this book in the good deeds and fatherly accomplishments of these amazing fathers. Some of them are members of my family; they all are a cross-section of what Black fatherhood really looks like across America.

For many of the men featured in this book, fatherhood is not merely a biological role, it is a sacred calling. It is a daily act of resistance against a world that too often tries to deny their humanity. To be a Black father is to carry the weight of history while planting seeds for a future that may never fully be realized. It is to teach children how to navigate systems designed to marginalize them, while also nurturing their joy, curiosity, and sense of self-worth.

Profoundly, some fathers' calling is not always fulfilled in traditional ways. Some fathers are present in the home, others are present through phone calls, prayers, and weekend visits. Some fathers through mentorship, through coaching, and through community engagement. Their presence is not confined to geography, it is measured in impact.

This book, above all, is dedicated to the Black father. However, it is also dedicated to the Black family, to the entire African American community. Years ago, I saw a video clip of our dear sister-scholar and literary giant, Toni Morrison, talking about the intended audience of her writings. In that clip, the interviewer asked if she could ever write for an audience other than a Black one. Her eloquent response, much more eloquent than I can ever be, aimed specifically at the Black reader. She talked about writing intentionally and intently for and from the African American lens. Ever since seeing that clip, I have adopted a similar, if the same, stance. Thus, this book is dedicated to Black perspective, to Black observation, to the Black gaze.

Like in previous publications, my primary goal is to assist the African American family — the collective Black consciousness — with seeing itself differently. For far too long, we have been subjected to a narrative about us that is far less than ideal or true about us. Public relations and advertising giant, Tom Burrell, would say that we have been subjected to a public relations campaign hell-bent on making us believe that we are inferior; that there has been a, several decades long, crusade trying to get us to believe that all of the negative things that have been said about us are true.[4]

One of my academic mentors always encouraged me to serve the community in some way. He specifically believed that our academic endeavors, our scholarly outputs, should be in service to the community. As a result of his advice, I have tried to leverage the skills that I've gained in the academy in service to my community. So again, my focus is on telling the truth about us—the Black community.

Finally, this book is dedicated to my future family members, primarily my unborn, not yet conceived grandchildren. But this book is also for my descendants who are decades, perhaps centuries, in the future. Throughout our time on American soil, the African American family has struggled to find our heritage, our lineage. Especially with regard to our ties to Mother Africa; the ties between us and Africa have almost completely been severed. We are privy to very little information about our African ancestors. Sure, we are just now beginning to discover more about who we were before we landed on American soil,[5] but we still have a lot of work to do. I want this book to serve as a breadcrumb for my descendants who will find themselves on the trail of self-discovery. I am certain that their quest will include a look into their past. I want them to find something there. So again, this book is dedicated to my unborn descendants.

Many of you may be familiar with Dr. Henry Lewis Gates, Jr's television show, *Finding Your Roots*. Well, I was watching the show one evening and Dr. Gates asked the featured guest a question that I had never heard anyone pose before. I don't remember, exactly, who the featured guest was that night, but I do remember the very profound question. Dr. Gates asked the guest, *"Do you know the African person who started your family's lineage on American soil?"* The question blew my mind. It was a question that I never considered for myself. Especially as a descendant of Georgetown, South Carolina, one of the port cities where enslaved Africans entered the country and where the presence of the formerly enslaved is still strongly felt, I instantly felt a tug in my soul. I felt a spark in my mind's eye.

After the show concluded, I dosed off to sleep in my favorite chair, thinking about that question, while trying to imagine that person — the African soul who started my family's lineage on American soil. In a dream, I saw him. He was bound in chains in the hull of a slave ship. Well, I believe that I saw him.

The next day, at work, I shared my dream experience with a colleague who studied philosophy and was nascently familiar with the study of metaphysics. He would often talk about the mysteries of our world, the relationship between time and space or what's real and what's imagined. His response to my dream experience was mind-blowing. He said, "Rodney, what if that really happened?" He went on the say, "We [humans] don't fully understand the power of God or the Universe. What if God allowed you to metaphysically travel through time to see your ancestor? What if your ancestor was praying that God would send him a sign to indicate that he would survive the months long trip across the Atlantic Ocean? What if you were his sign that he, indeed, was going to survive the trip?"

I share that story to highlight the fact that I really don't know who my African ancestors are. Those connections have been severed by the institution of slavery and by time. Though I will likely engage in some sort of genealogy search at some point in my life, at the moment, I have very few breadcrumbs to help me trace my way back to my ancestors. So again, this book is a breadcrumb for my descendants.

Chapter Summaries

So, what should you expect to find in this book? In the upcoming pages, you will find a narrative that defies the common stereotypes that you have heard about Black fathers. You will read the real-life testimonies of fathers who live out the true meaning of fatherhood on a daily basis. You will bear witness to both their trials and triumphs. You will also discover the origins of this age-old myth, an untruth that has, long, claimed that African American fathers are absent. In this book, you are being made privy to a counter-narrative, a profound truth about Black fathers that contradicts what you have, no doubt, been led to believe. If you have ever taken as truth any of the lies told about Black fathers, at the conclusion of this book, hopefully your beliefs will change. The details of each chapter are provided in the summaries below:

Chapter 1, "A Man Made of Steel" is about my dad. He has simply been the epitome of fatherhood. The chapter explicitly highlights the parallels between my dad's work as a steelmaker in my hometown and his years of fatherly mentorship in that same town. It starts with a description of the earliest days of the town, when the work of enslaved Africans helped to make the region one of the wealthiest regions in colonial America.[6] The chapter connects the dots between the strength and character that established my hometown and the strength and character of my dad.

The chapter then turns to highlight some of the life lessons and nuggets of wisdom that my dad passed on to us when we were growing up. This section of the chapter reads like a memoir, where I share stories of my youth and of my dad's permeating presence in our lives. I tell stories about how my dad taught us lessons about bullying, leadership, character, politics and a host of other valuable life principles. The chapter closes talking about the significance and importance of a father's role in a child's life. The chapter declares that a present and engaged father helps to establish a child's emotional stability, self-esteem, and social development. Alongside mothers, fathers bring a different set of emotional responses to situations that occur in a child's life, causing the child to develop a well-rounded understanding of him or herself as well as a good understanding of the world around them. Fathers help to create children who are well-adjusted, emotionally, socially and psychologically.

Chapter 2, "The Fathers in my Family", highlights a few fathers who have been major influences in my life. They are glowing examples of what Black fatherhood is and has been forever in this country. The chapter specifically highlights my fathers-in-law, my wife's biological father, and her bonus dad. They both have been pillars of love and strength in my life. The chapter opens with stories about how both of them embraced me from the very start of my relationship with their daughter and how they have been supportive throughout. The chapter then features a few gentlemen whom I have looked up to and have gained strength and wisdom over the years. This includes my brother-in-law, Troy, who has fathered a number of children who are not his own, biologically. I describe him as *The Father* of his small village.

I conclude the chapter featuring two of my relatives. One of my relatives is a 23-year-old single father who has assumed sole custody of his one-year-old son. He completely shatters the negative narratives and stereotypes that are said about African American fathers. He, along with a supportive village of family members, including his twin sister, is navigating the earliest phase of his son's life. He is determined to be a major part of helping to write the first chapters of his son's earthly journey.

The relative that completes this chapter of amazing fathers is one of the people who has been closest to me my entire life. He is my brother, Eric C. Smith. His story, in many regards, is painful, but in the end, it is extremely inspiring. He is incarcerated but somehow has managed to stay connected and engaged in his children's lives. It is a testament to the notion that love, combined with intentionality, can conquer circumstances, distance, as well as physical boundaries. His story is also a demonstration of the often-referenced bible verse, Proverbs 13:22, which says that "a good man leaves an inheritance to his children's children." His inheritance, which is an inheritance that we share, comes from our father's good deeds and faithfulness to his family. The strength of our father's love and commitment to the family is helping to keep, not just my brother whole, but the entire family whole.

Chapter 3, "My Friends are Great Fathers." This chapter is the result of interviews, both individual interviews and group interviews, that I conducted with some of my close friends and acquaintances. They are real-life examples of fatherhood in action. More than a few scholars have concluded that Black fathers are just as active, and in many cases more active, than fathers from other ethnic and racial groups.[7] The gentlemen highlighted in this chapter are tangible examples of the aforementioned data.

Emerging from the interviews are seven themes that personify fatherhood. Each theme is not only listed and defined, but each theme is also accompanied by direct quotes from the fathers who participated in the interviews. The quotes attempt to capture the fundamental essence of the themes. The quotes are a kind of color commentary that helps to crystallize the in-depth meaning of the theme.

In the end, the chapter authenticates several qualities about Black men and Black fathers that have long been misconstrued. In order to arrive at the themes featured in this chapter, the fathers who were interviewed had to tap into a level of intimacy and vulnerability that is not commonly seen in men. The conversations that produced these themes were open, honest, and sincere. They required a kind of emotional openness that is rare. The men featured in this chapter defy the stereotypes that are both said and believed about men, and especially Black men. Perhaps most importantly, they provided real-life evidence and examples of what committed and engaged fatherhood looks like. They are the complete opposite of what America has defined as a "deadbeat." They are truly antithetical to the myth.

Chapter 4, "The Truth about Black Fathers" starts with an examination of the history that produced the myth of the "absent Black father." The chapter takes a close look at American Chattel Slavery, the historically discriminatory policies and practices of the United States, and the distorted media depictions of the entire Black family but pays special attention to the portrayal of Black fathers. The chapter names the United States government and, specifically, the U.S. Department of Labor's role in perpetuating this lie about the Black father's so-called absence. A 1965 governmentally sanctioned document commonly referred to as the Moynihan Report is mentioned throughout this chapter, highlighting its significance in promulgating the myth. The document was written by the Assistant Secretary of Labor, a young politician of Irish descent named Daniel Patrick Moynihan. He served under the Lyndon B. Johnson administration.

The chapter then pivots to focus on the outcomes of what the research community has been saying about Black Fatherhood. Scholars have long claimed that Black fathers are not as disengaged as was once believed. A few pivotal studies are offered as empirical evidence that Black fathers are, indeed, present in their children's lives. In some cases, Black fathers are more engaged than White fathers and Hispanic fathers. A 2023 study entitled, *The Myth of Low-Income Black Fathers' Absence From the Lives of Adolescents*, solicited the voices of teenagers with Black fathers to gain their perspective on how close they felt to and how engaged they believed their fathers are in their lives. The results prove that Black fathers are no less engaged than fathers from other ethnic groups.[8]

The chapter closes after introducing a group of fathers who

are rarely, if ever, mentioned when the subject of fatherhood is broached. A 2021 study entitled, *A Portrait of Caring Black Men*, introduces fathers who are *High-Intensity Caregivers and/or Parents* (HICP). They are defined as "people who [have] ever provided care to an adult family member or a friend who has or has had a serious illness or disability AND/OR parents who have ever cared for a child under 18 with a medical or behavioral condition or disability (i.e. special need)".[9]

Chapter 5, "The Conclusion" ties the misnomer of the missing Black father back to the community that is affected most—the Black community. The chapter highlights the significance and importance of the Black women who stands alongside the Black man. It rehashes, then debunks the old trope that Black men are an endangered species. It concludes that extinction is, ultimately, not possible because of the presence and power of Black women.

The chapter wraps up dreaming of a better America. It casts a vision where Black fathers are treated equitably and with dignity. It imagines a portrayal of America where Black children grow up in communities with their fathers present, and their fathers are leading by example. It envisions an America where Black men are not disproportionately targeted by the criminal legal system. The chapter conceives an America where job creation and opportunities are made available equitably in Black communities and neighborhoods, just as they have been plentiful in other communities.

Ultimately, the chapter suggests that until this is realized with and for the Black community, America will not have fulfilled its promise. The chapter supposes that our country, as great as it is, will not reach its fullest potential without the full participation of all of its citizens. The chapter argues that America is disallowing, and in many respects, thwarting its own progress. If America is going to be the place of freedom, liberty and justice that it proclaims to be, then the Black family should be raised to its rightful place. And with the Black man, and the Black father specifically, serving as the head of the Black family, his image must be depicted as it truly is; essential, powerful and worthy.

Chapter 6, "What Should We (You) Do Next" encourages action. It reminds us that readers should not stop after reading this book but urges readers to *Support Black Fathers Through Policy and Advocacy, Mentor the Next Generation, Build Community, Change the Narrative and Become the Family's Griot*. The chapter, in the end, is a call to action. It challenges inactivity while promoting activism.

This book is a counter-narrative. It directly confronts and attempts to dismantle the myth of the absent Black father. It blends historical context, data, and provides a cultural analysis in an effort to disassemble this long-standing stereotype.

The myth of the absent Black father is not just a lie, it has been used as a weapon. It has been used to justify punitive policies, to stigmatize entire communities, and to erode the self-image of Black folk, and perhaps most detrimentally within Black children. It suggests that Black men are inherently irresponsible, emotionally unavailable, and incapable of nurturing. These misnomers ignore systemic barriers like mass incarceration, economic disenfranchisement, and racial profiling; the societal factors that have made fatherhood more difficult, not less valued.

And yet, Black fathers persist. We build mettle with the faith and wisdom of our fathers and grandfathers. We show up in ways that defy statistics and stereotypes. We pass down metaphysical heirlooms, lessons of dignity, resilience, and spiritual grounding that cannot be measured by census data or media soundbites.

To honor Black fatherhood is to tell the truth. It is to elevate stories of sacrifice, tenderness, and wisdom. It is to recognize that Black fathers are not anomalies, we are architects of hope. We are not absent. We are often unseen. We are not broken. We are builders.

The new narrative, that I hope this book helps to usher in, must be rooted in truth and love. It must show Black fathers not as footnotes in our children's lives, but as authors of generational transformation. It must celebrate the fullness of our presence.

As you read through the pages of this book, I invite you to recall the fathers and father-figures in your life. Even if your biological father was not a part of your life, I suspect that there was someone (or several individuals) who provided fatherly advice and offered a fatherly presence in your life. Think of the people who showed up with steadiness when you needed stability, who challenged you when you needed growth, and who believed in you before you fully believed in yourself. These figures, whether relatives, mentors, coaches, elders in your community, or everyday heroes in your neighborhood, helped to shape the contours of who you are today. Their influence may not have always been perfect or even perceptible to the naked eye, but it was often purposeful. And in reflecting on them, we not only honor their impact but also recognize the ways we, too, are called to offer guidance, protection, and love to those who look to us. My hope is that this book will help you see the threads of fatherhood, both given and received, that have woven strength, wisdom, and resilience into your story.

A Note on Racial Terminology

As in prior publications, you will notice that I capitalize the racial terms “Black” and “White” throughout the entire book. I do this as a measure of fairness, consistency, and equality. The term “Black” is capitalized because it is an acknowledgement that it represents more than just a skin color. It represents a shared culture, a historical as well as a social experience. It honors the legacy of African descendants in America, including the resilience spawned by American Chattel Slavery, racial segregation and systemic oppression. Similarly, I capitalize the term “White” as a matter of consistency when referring to racial groups. Capitalizing both terms helps to level the playing field of linguistics and literary meaning.

CHAPTER ONE

A MAN MADE OF STEEL

"The power of a dad in a child's life is unmatched."
Justin Ricklefs

The title of this book derives from the fact that my father is a retired steelworker. But, most importantly, the title intends to suggest that my dad has been, not just our hero, but our superhero. He has been a major influence in the lives of both of his biological children (my brother and me), in the lives of my two cousins (more like sisters) as well as in the lives of others who are of no biological relation. My dad worked as a steelworker for nearly 40 years in our small hometown, Georgetown, South Carolina.

Noteworthily, Georgetown is the third oldest city and the second largest port city in the state, second to Charleston, South Carolina. It is a significant part of what is known as the Lowcountry and the Gullah Geechee region of South Carolina. During its earliest years, Georgetown is where enslaved Africans cultivated half of the United States' rice production. The Africans who were brought to the region were intentionally selected for their expertise in the art and science of growing rice. They came from West African countries like Angola, Ghana, Nigeria, Senegal, Sierra Leone and others with climates and terrains similar to that of South Carolina. They were smart and strong people whose intelligence and ingenuity made Georgetown the richest city in the state and contributed to South Carolina being one of the wealthiest colonies during the colonial period of this country.[1]

I mention these facts about Georgetown because, hopefully, they give you a sense of the strength and determination that permeates the place where my dad was born and raised, and still now lives. His upbringing as well as mine mirrors the production of steel in many respects.

Interestingly, iron is the primary substance used in the creation of steel.[2] This fact causes me to immediately recall a common phrase that I have heard throughout my life, that "iron sharpens iron." The notion of iron sharpening iron speaks to the mutual growth that transpires when two individuals are in a healthy and productive relationship. Growth is definitely what we gained as a result of our interactions with my dad. I say we because, as alluded to earlier, my dad has had a profound influence on a number of my friends and extended family members in addition to the influence that he has had on me.

I am no metallurgist, but I have come to realize that steel is actually a stronger version of its base metal, iron. Steel is an alloy metal that is created as a result of mixing iron with carbon. By simply adding carbon to iron, iron becomes a stronger version of itself. [3] This is an extremely powerful point to consider, the fact that by adding carbon, iron becomes a more durable substance than when it is in its original state. Comparing the process of steelmaking with the growth and development of human beings, more specifically, with the growth and development of those of us who have been influenced by my dad, one can see the similarities. My dad has been making steel in two parallel ways. He has been making steel as a result of his years of employment in the steel mill in our hometown and also by adding a bit of his love and attention to us, he has been helping to create strong and productive human beings.

What makes steel remarkable is not just its strength, but its versatility—its ability to be both firm and flexible when needed.[4] My dad in many respects embodies these qualities. He maintains unwavering principles while showing remarkable adaptability. In other words, he has always maintained a demeanor that is warm, kind and approachable, while upholding a sense of dignity and self-respect. Throughout life, he rarely showed anger or agitation toward us, however, there were times when if we violated one of life's important principles, he would get on us pretty hard. This point reminds me of a time during my youth when I played junior varsity football.

Leaders Build Confidence

On this particular day, my dad was sitting in his car waiting for us after football practice. As we were approaching my dad's car, I was "jawing" back and forth with a teammate about how good I was and how "sorry" he was in comparison to me. While friendly banter and machismo are common among male athletes, my dad didn't tolerate the kind of banter or machismo that infringed on being a good teammate and team leader. When we finally got in the car, my dad gave me one of those looks that a father gives when his emotions are somewhere between disappointment and "pisstivity." His displeased facial expression was accompanied by the following words, "You need to learn how to shut your big mouth." In his opinion, I was getting the bighead in addition to being a horrible team leader.

As the starting quarterback for my team, he believed that I should be spending my energy encouraging my teammates as opposed to degrading them. We spent the car ride home with him reminding me and my friends that football is a team sport and that no one player is better than the sum of the whole team, and that my banter with my teammate was an indication that I was a poor team leader. I didn't fully understand his point at the time, but I have learned, along the way, that my dad was absolutely correct. Good leaders are those who create confidence in those who are being led. They build people up as opposed to tearing them down.

My dad also stood firm in other ways in the community. As you can probably imagine from my description of Georgetown in an earlier part of this chapter, that the town has had its share of racial issues and incidents over the years, some subtle and some, not so subtle. With a history like ours, it is not hard to imagine that race and its concomitant challenges would rear its ugly head from time to time in our small town. Well, the story below is one such time.

Standing Up for Others

My high school, Georgetown High School, was established in 1984. Prior to its founding the city laid claim to two distinct high schools, Howard High School, a predominantly Black high school on the city's west side and Winyah High School, a predominantly White high school on the east side of town. Howard High School's official colors were Royal Blue and Old Gold, while Winyah's school colors were Crimson and Cream. *I think the official colors were actually Red and White, but Crimson and Cream sounds more descriptive to me.* When the two schools merged to create Georgetown High, the community agreed that the new school's colors would be completely distinct from any of the two previous schools' colors. The community selected Navy and Gray. All sports apparel and paraphernalia would be Navy and Gray.

Leading up to the 87-88 football season, our head coach instructed the team to remove the school's gray decal from our navy helmets and informed us that we were getting a new decal. After removing the decal, our excitement grew as we anticipated the new decal that would soon adorn our helmets. Would it be a ferocious looking bulldog, our school's mascot or would it be a giant letter G for Georgetown? We couldn't wait to see the new decal.

A few days would pass before our coach would distribute the new decal. Much to our dismay, the new decal was a giant "red" G. Many of us immediately began to voice our disappointment in the fact that the decal was a departure from the community's wishes. Some of us saw it as a subtle acknowledgement of Winyah High School, and thus an affirming gesture to the White community while simultaneously disregarding the Black community.

By this time, I was driving myself and a few of my

teammates to and from practice, so we didn't have my dad immediately there to help us process our thoughts and feelings. But, as soon as we got to my house, we jumped out of the car and ran in to inform my dad. He heard our disappointment in the fact that the decal was red and represented a departure from the community's initial agreement. Like always, he helped us process our feelings of disappointment and told us to remain focused on being the best team and teammates to and for each other.

A few days later, seemingly out of nowhere, our coach instructed us to remove the red decal from our helmets. We followed instructions just like we had done before, but this time we were confused. We were perplexed as to why we were being asked to remove the decal just days after having been instructed to put them on our helmets. It would be weeks later that we discovered that my dad had quietly pulled a few strings in the community to have the decal removed, stating that the decal was a departure from what the community had agreed upon.

I learned something from my dad in that situation, he demonstrated that true strength does not lie in simply being resistant to change but is built in the ability to stand your ground and stand on your word, and in gently helping others to honor their word too. I also learned that leadership is much more about disposition than it is about position. As you know by now, my dad was "just" a concerned community member who worked in our town's steel mill. He wasn't an elected official or a clergyperson championing the concerns of his constituents. He was, however, a father protecting the interests of his kids.

As teenagers, we didn't have the power or the know-how to inspire our school to keep its word with regard to the school's colors, but my dad did. Ultimately, I learned that one of the duties of a father is to serve as an advocate for his children. A father speaks up for his children when they can't speak up for themselves. Again, like steel, my dad was firm, but also pliable seemingly simultaneously. This causes me to recall a lesson about bullying that my dad taught us when we were kids.

Standing Up for Yourself

The neighborhood I grew up in was a pretty close-knit group of families, with multiple children in each household during the 1970s and 80s. In fact, my family was a relatively small unit in comparison to some of the other families in our neighborhood. My family was made up of my dad, mom, brother and me. There were more than a few families with a dad, mom and four (sometimes more) children. Because there were so many kids in the neighborhood, we played outside together daily.

For the boys in the neighborhood, our game of choice was "Throw-Up Tackle" also known as "Kill the Man with the Ball". I have also heard the game referred to as "Pick-up Smith". It's a game where we would all gather in a tight circle and someone would toss a football into the air, much like the referees toss a basketball in the air at the tip-off of a basketball game. The entire group, regardless of the size of the group, would then try to tackle the person who caught the ball. I know that it sounds dangerous (because it was), but it was the source of tons of fun when we were young.

My brother was a fairly big guy compared to the rest of us guys in our age range. *His nickname until today is "Bigum".* So, needless to say, it would be virtually impossible to tackle him during a game of "Throw-Up Tackle". Because of this, a few of the guys would coerce—in a lot of cases—bully my brother into giving up the ball when he caught it. Because my brother was a relatively gentle kid, he would give the ball up. Unfortunately, the bullying would extend outside of the game of "Throw-up Tackle" and became almost an everyday occurrence. As the little brother, of course, I wanted to do something to help defend my brother, but due to size, age, and stature I was often unsuccessful in my efforts. Coincidentally, my dad found out about the bullying.

In an effort to teach my brother how to defend himself against being bullied and to stop our friend Stephon* *(named changed to protect identity)* from getting too far down the road of being a bully, my dad made my brother defend himself one day. It was a Sunday afternoon, and we were out in the front yard playing "Throw-up Tackle."

My dad had obviously been keeping an eye on us from his usual spot on the couch while watching Sunday afternoon football. Like many times before, the bullying started. As things progressed, we all noticed that my dad had come outside and was making his way toward us. We had somehow managed to wander out into the street by this time. We assumed that my dad was there to stop the minor pushing and shoving that was taking place. Much to our surprise, my dad briefly separated Eric and Stephon, and then instructed my brother to defend himself from being bullied. My brother awkwardly got into a boxing stance with his left arm somewhat extended, *this is an important detail because my brother is left-hand dominant.* Stephon also awkwardly got into a boxing stance and thus the kid street boxing match ensued.

As you can probably imagine, Stephon and Eric circled each other several times with fists drawn before taking a swing. After a few circles around, someone from the small gathering of neighborhood boys yelled, “swing.” Stephon swung and missed and then Eric swung and missed. This went on for a few more seconds and then Eric landed a vicious left hook to the right side of Stephon’s face. I still remember seeing sweat violently leave Stephon’s face as he stumbled back and was visibly dazed from the blow. If my dad hadn’t been there to catch him, he would have surely fell to the ground. It seemed like there was an unspoken consensus among the group, including my dad, that Stephon had had enough with the one singular blow, and just as awkwardly as the boxing match started, it had now ended.

Not much was said after the incident, we all went to our respective homes rather quietly. My dad, Eric and I didn’t say much to each other once in the house either. In many respects, I think we were a bit stunned by what had just happened and were processing in our own ways. In retrospect, I imagine my dad was wondering if he had done the right thing or at least had done it the right way. I imagine my brother was rejoicing a bit, internally. I was rejoicing too, for my brother, and simultaneously wondering what would happen the next time we played “Throw-up Tackle” or the next time we saw Stephon in the neighborhood.

I recognize that physical force and/or aggression is not necessarily the preferred method that one should employ when defending oneself. Some of you may even disagree with my father's approach to teaching a lesson about bullying. Nevertheless, I believe that my father's method in that era was an approach that was universally understood. Like it or not, boys in the 1970s and 80s often settled our differences in fisticuffs.

Trust and Protection

My father was also really cool and easy-going when it came to us hanging out and having fun with our friends in the neighborhood. One time that sticks out in my head is Halloween. I don't remember the specific year, but I remember the occasion. With so many kids in the neighborhood, Halloween was always a really big deal in our neighborhood. Our streets would be packed with trick-or-treaters going door to door as soon as the sun set. Because our neighborhood was such a close-knit community, when we got to middle school age, our parents allowed us to go trick-or-treating without their direct supervision. This was a big deal. I vividly remember the sense of freedom I felt when we were allowed to trick-or-treat by ourselves. Because of this new freedom and because of our excitement, we left the house really early on this particular Halloween to join our friends. Because we left the house so early and to honor our newfound privilege, we returned a bit early. When we arrived, my dad still had our porch light on indicating that he was still passing out candy to trick-or-treaters. I explicitly remember this Halloween, because my mom was typically in charge of all Halloween activities, but for some reason, my dad was subbing in for her this particular year. We rang our own doorbell like we were trick-or-treaters. My dad came to the door and gave us candy like he had done for countless other kids in the neighborhood. He then asked us a couple of questions that blew our minds, "Are you guys done with trick-or-treating already?" "Do you want to go back out for more?" Beaming with even more excitement, we quickly dumped our bags of candy on the kitchen table so my dad could inspect our first batch and quickly headed back out the door for a second round of trick-or-treating. We were on cloud nine.

Notice that I said that my dad was going to inspect our treats. Yes, that's correct, my parents would always inspect our treats for foreign objects that could harm us, if consumed. I am not sure if it was just an urban legend, but we often heard of objects like shards of glass or small blades being placed in treats like fruit and candy bars, so my parents would always examine our treats. Funny thing, I found myself doing the same thing after becoming a parent. When my kids returned home from trick-or-treating, I would always examine their treats. It goes without saying that the protection of our children is a father's number one priority.

Compassion and Empathy

Another occasion that sticks out in my mind is one of the four times that it snowed in Georgetown during my childhood. That's right, you read that correctly, it snowed a total of four times during my entire childhood. In fact, as I write these words, snow is on the ground in my hometown after nearly 35 years of any significant snowfall.[5] So, needless to say, snow in my hometown was and still is a really big deal.

Because it snowed so infrequently, we were beyond excited to get out and play in the snow. This particular time, there was only about an inch of snow, so we were still scheduled to attend school for a half-day. To give the snow a chance to melt, we were to report to school at noon, which gave my friends and I ample time to play in the snow. My dad's instructions were to play in the snow, but to be mindful not to get my clothes too wet as I would wear those same clothes to school. You guessed it, I got completely drenched from head to toe.

My dad was upset, but not to the point where I got in any serious trouble. He grumbled a bit but then helped me change out of my wet clothes in time to catch the bus for school. I think he understood my excitement about the snow and gave me a pass for my unintentional disobedience.

My dad has never really been a physically affectionate guy. He showed his tenderness and affection by being very understanding of us and our youthful blunders. He never really overreacted to our slip-ups. As I mentioned earlier, he would get on us if and when we violated one of life's important principles, but he never made a big deal of our innocent mistakes.

Without slipping into hyperbole, these kinds of moments with my dad taught me lessons about compassion and empathy. When my dad showed empathy and understanding toward our mishaps and mistakes, he was in essence, modeling compassion for us. Looking back on those moments, I now realize that I was learning how to be understanding and empathetic toward others. I also believe that those moments strengthened my relationship with my dad. With him being supportive and non-judgmental of my many mistakes, my connection and trust in him was strengthened. Those moments created a safe space for open communication and mutual respect. Ultimately, those moments resulted in heightened self-esteem and confidence for me. When caring adults show understanding and forgiveness of youthful mistakes, young people feel both supported and valued, which enables them to take on new challenges with confidence and optimism.[6] I have not always succeeded in this area with my children, but I am vowing to do better.

Shaping the Future

My dad was and still is our family's griot. In West African cultures, the griot is the village's storyteller, historian, and keeper of oral traditions. The griot plays a significant role in African and African American communities, as they help to preserve history, culture and the traditions of their communities. They are often described as living libraries. They pass down cultural knowledge and family folklore through the generations using narratives and storytelling. They serve as advisors and mediators within their families and communities. They also have a way of predicting the future, by highlighting significant moments from the past.[7] Make no mistake about it, the tradition of the griot is still alive and well today, and continues to be a significant part of African American families through people like my dad.

Some of my most fond memories trace back to family gatherings where we sat around listening to my dad tell stories about his childhood and early adult life. In fact, I truly believe that I am now an educator and scholar because of one of those stories. The story was a simple, seemingly insignificant account of my dad coming home from work one evening when we lived in West Philadelphia. I was too young to remember much about our lives in Philadelphia, but I know, through stories, that our house was not far from the University of Pennsylvania's campus. My dad tells this story of him walking near campus on his way home from work and inadvertently bumping into a UPenn student. Because of how my dad was dressed on this particular evening, the student assumed that he was a professor and said "excuse me professor" when their shoulders touched. *(I guess professors dressed more formally back then.)* When my dad told this story, he told it with such reverence and admiration for the title of professor, I believe that it stuck with me, causing me to think of the title in the same way. In fact, I know that my dad has always held education and educators in high regard. I recall him advising me to select education as my major when I was heading off to college. Inexplicably, I did not take my dad's advice initially, I majored in Architecture as an undergraduate instead. Interestingly though, as fate would have it, my master's and doctoral degrees are both in the field of education. I guess the old adage that "father knows best" is indeed an adage for a reason. I suppose that my father knew something about me that I had yet to realize about myself. Interestingly, my dad also suggested that I consider politics as a potential career choice.

My dad has always held a high regard for engaging in the political process. My first experience dealing with politics was as a youth when my dad would load my friends and me in his car and drive us around our neighborhood and adjacent neighborhoods to distribute political literature during election season. We would sometimes gripe about politics, stating that it was a corrupt industry. He would always say that politics doesn't have to be corrupt, that mankind had somehow veered away from the true meaning of politics. My dad had somehow discovered, throughout his life experiences, what ancient Africans intended when they established centralized kingdoms, chiefdoms and empires via the use of collectivism, with a strong emphasis on community participation and engagement.[8] My dad had discovered that politics, in its purest form, was more about caring for your neighbor than it is about power and control. He has always regarded politics as a means to enhance community relationships which results in increased community harmony.

I share these thoughts about politics because, recently, I have been contemplating the idea of serving on the school board in the district where my children attended school. It's an elected position, which in the end is both a political and educational position. Either my dad could see my future, or he was shaping it. I think it was a bit of both. He saw the kind of person I was becoming and began to coach me in that direction.

Again, stories like these don't seem significant, but are quite impactful when we take the time to really think about them. I think the bigger story is the fact that, throughout my upbringing, I had spent so much time with my dad that he knew my innate gifts and talents, and I knew the nuances of how he thought, and thus, absorbed what was important to him. That could not have happened if my dad wasn't a significant part of my life. My dad was and still is a ubiquitous presence in my life. My dad's presence in my life has caused me to strive to do the same for my children. I pride myself on being an everyday, all-day, full-time, hands-on father.

Later in this book, you will discover that most of my friends and acquaintances are everyday, all-day, full-time, hands-on fathers as well. I interviewed several of my friends in preparation for this book, and to a person, they all, at some point in our conversations, talked about the importance of spending time with their children. It's an important aspect of fatherhood.

A Coach and Mentor

When I was young, my father was the dad in the neighborhood who would drive my friends and me to our Pop Warner Football practices and games. He wouldn't stop there but would then volunteer as a coach. He wasn't just a coach in title, he was a mentor to every kid on the field. He taught us not only the rules of the game but also the values of teamwork, perseverance, and sportsmanship. His dedication was often recognized with volunteer coaching trophies at the end of the season, but the real reward was in the lessons we learned and the bonds we formed. This is made evident in the fact that many of the friends I mention earlier are still my friends today and most still maintain a distinct relationship with my dad or should I say, our dad.

Admittedly, my father's active presence in our lives was a bit atypical for men from his generation. My dad was born in 1941; he is from the Silent Generation. While most men in his generation were hard workers and great providers, a lot of them were present in the home, but relatively silent when it came to their involvement in the extracurricular activities of their children. Consequently, most of the homes in my neighborhood had fathers present, but a lot of the fathers were not as active as my father was in their children's extracurricular activities.

As alluded to earlier, my neighborhood was an all-Black community with very little involvement from other communities outside of ours. Of course, we went to school with kids from all over our small town, but like a lot of neighborhoods in the 1970s and 80s, our neighborhood was quite intimate and inwardly facing. In other words, everyone knew everyone. This made my dad's presence even more impactful. In fact, some of the other fathers willingly relied on my dad to assist with their children's extracurricular activities. As a result and as I mentioned above, many of my friends maintain a relationship with my dad today because of his involvement in their lives back then.

I recently learned that a really close childhood friend would call my parents just to comfort himself when he was away at war during Operation Desert Storm. He would purposely call my mom and dad when his parents weren't available. He credits my parents, my dad specifically, with helping to keep him alive while away at war.

I learned from another close friend that my dad would

always slip him a few dollars for his pocket when he visited us while we were away in college. Interestingly, that same friend's father would do the same for me when he visited. Neither of us knew that our fathers were doing that for each other.

A Father's Role

Overarchingly, the role of a father is significant in the life of a child; fathers play a crucial role in the development of their children. Their influence extends beyond just financial support, they offer emotional guidance, help to establish boundaries, and model appropriate behaviors. The emotional bond between a father and his children can be foundational to their children's lives. Fathers who are actively involved in their children's lives contribute to their emotional stability, self-esteem, and social development.[9] As I have mentioned throughout this chapter, my father's abounding presence in my life has definitely contributed to the successes I've experienced in life.

I believe that the involvement of fathers, like my dad, help to change the image of fathers overarchingly. In our current society, there is and has been, especially in the last 30 years, growing expectations as well as emphasis on fathers being active and engaged, breaking away from traditional stereotypes. Fathers today are more involved in daily parenting activities and share responsibilities along with mothers. [10] As well, the influence of fatherhood extends beyond the family unit to society at large. Fathers who are positive role models contribute to the development of responsible, empathetic, and resilient future generations.[11] Their impact is felt in communities, workplaces, and beyond.

My life has truly been blessed by the involvement of my father. Remarkably, my life has also been blessed by the presence of additional father-figures like both of my fathers-in-law. My wife's biological father and her bonus father have both added tremendous value to my life. They both have always treated me like their own from day one. Looking back over the twenty-four years that my wife and I have been married, I can practically count the good fortune they have brought to my life.

In the next chapter, I will highlight my fathers-in-law and a few additional amazing fathers who are a part of my family and extended family. They are a cross-section of what Black fatherhood really looks like in America. They all are a combination of love, affection and action in the lives of their children. Interestingly, one of the fathers I mention in the next chapter has bigheartedly parented children who are not his own biologically, which is much more common in the Black community than generally believed.[12] Again, these gentlemen are stellar examples of what Black fatherhood looks like in America.

All-in-all, fatherhood is a lifelong journey filled with ups and downs, challenges, and rewards. By embracing your role as a father, you can make a lasting and positive impact on your children's lives and on society as a whole. The community is watching both directly and indirectly. There are young people who are a part of your life, some you know personally, and others are on the periphery of your life, all of them needing your fatherly presence. I know without a shadow of a doubt that I am the father that I am today because of the influence of my father and other father-figures who modeled for me what fatherhood should be. We must do and be the same for the young people in our lives today.

CHAPTER TWO

THE FATHERS IN MY FAMILY

"It is not flesh and blood but the heart which makes us fathers and sons"
Friedrich von Schiller

My Father-in-law, Ullyses

My wife's family originates in a small Black town in Oklahoma called Boley. Every year during the Memorial Day holiday weekend, we travel there for the Boley Rodeo.[1] The gathering is more than just a rodeo, it is a time for families and friends to come together to celebrate life and to celebrate each other. My father-in-law, Ullyses' family typically hosts a huge gathering of family and friends, where we come together under an assembly of tents for food and fun. During one of my earlier gatherings as a new family member, I met one of my father-in-law's lifelong friends for the first time. I assume that he knew about our marriage but simply hadn't had the chance to meet me.

Picture the setting; my father-in-law was sitting at a table playing dominoes with three of his brothers as other family members engaged in a variety of family activities — music, children playing, food, games, and lots of laughter. My father-in-law's friend, Skipper, was making his way through the assembly of tents greeting various family members. When he got to me, he stopped and leaned in to shake my hand and said, "I don't remember meeting this family member. Whose son is this?". Almost in unison, several family members yelled, "that's Stephenie's husband." He repeated "Stephenie's husband?", with the voice intonation of a question-like statement. He then tapped my father-in-law on the shoulder and asked, "who is this guy?" while pointing in my direction. He wasn't being mean but was simply engaging in the kind of sarcastic ribbing that takes place when a male family member meets the significant other of a female family member for the first time. My father-in-law turned around to see that he was gesturing toward me and said, "oh, that's my son."

I can't fully describe the feeling I had when my father-in-law said those words. It was a combination of surprise, relief and jubilation. It was euphoric. To have my father-in-law claim me in such a way and to publicly endorse my relationship with his daughter meant the world to me. It said to me that he believed in me and in our marriage, and that he loved me too.

My father-in-law has been in my corner from day one of my relationship with his daughter, Stephenie. He has been a symbol of strength and has been the embodiment of belief in our marriage. As a matter of fact, I can clearly recall the day that I asked him for Stephenie's hand in marriage. In fact, the day that I asked for her hand wasn't exactly the ideal day to do so. To be even more frank, it was one of those days that my soon-to-be wife and I weren't seeing eye to eye. However, the conversation with my father-in-law helped to regulate my thoughts and, in many respects, served as confirmation that I was indeed making the right decision. He spoke life into me on that day. I remember him telling me that he was impressed with me, that he was especially impressed with how I had "hit the ground running" after completing college, that I was "taking life by the horn." He said that he felt secure in allowing his daughter to marry someone like me and proceeded to warmly grant me permission to ask Stephenie for her hand in marriage. He has been extremely supportive of me and our marriage since that day.

He has also given me a glimpse of what life might be like as a father to an adult daughter. Our daughter Phoenix is now 24 years old and forging a new life independent of our everyday guidance as her parents, so I've been relying on the example of other fathers who have already successfully navigated those waters. My father-in-law is an up-close and personal example of how things may look. He engages with my wife and her two sisters, Trina and Regan, from what I would describe as an appropriate fatherly distance.

Ever since I can remember, he has had a weekly call, typically on Sundays, with Stephenie just to check-in and talk about family updates and anything else that's going on in the world. It is an aspect of their relationship that I have appreciated and admired, and serves as an approach that we have emulated in our relationship with Phoenix and our son Chi, for that matter.

I also remember when we were in the throes of house hunting and pondering the decision to purchase the house that we ultimately bought, my father-in-law's advice helped us to, in the end, make the leap. We brought him with us one afternoon to do a walkthrough of the property, and after thoroughly examining the property, he turned to me and said the following words, "you all will positively affect the trajectory of your children's lives, by raising them in a home like this." We made the purchase and have now carved out a pretty amazing life, in large part because of his fatherly advice and perspective. He even helped us with the initial down payment.

An added bonus to my relationship with my father-in-law is the fact that he and my father have developed a relationship of their own and have become really good friends. Quite frequently, I will receive a call from my dad telling me that my father-in-law just called him or in some cases, that he had just stopped by my parents' home during one of his many trips to South Carolina's low country. It warms my heart to know that these two very important men in my life share a bond of friendship.

My Father-in-law, Mike

You may have noticed that in an earlier part of this chapter, I mentioned that I am blessed to have two fathers-in-law. My father-in-law, Mike, Stephenie's bonus dad, rounds out the circle of immediate fathers that I have in my life. He and my mother-in-law, Beverly, have been and still are staples in our lives. Like my father-in-law Ullyses, Mike too, has been a huge support and has been in my corner from day one of my relationship with Stephenie. I actually recall the day that I met him.

Stephenie and I had traveled to Kansas City from Nashville to visit her mom, who was briefly hospitalized at the time. Mike was warm and welcoming and treated me like family immediately. I explicitly remember when Stephenie and I were preparing to drive back to Nashville, he and my mother-in-law insisted on giving us their car, a brand-new Honda Accord, in exchange for Stephenie's early 1990's, S Series Saturn, a car that she bought from a used car lot in Nashville. While we owned a two-seater sports car that I purchased back when I lived in Atlanta, the Honda Accord would serve as our first family car in Nashville. It was the car that we drove our 1st born, Phoenix, home in after birth. In fact, it was the car that I drove back to Kansas City nine years later, when we decided to move to Kansas City. That car, in many respects, serves as the foundation of my relationship with Mike.

Another memory that sticks out in my mind is one of the many times that Mike and my mother-in-law traveled to Nashville to visit. This particular time, they were there to celebrate Thanksgiving with us. For the family's Thanksgiving meal, Mike was responsible for preparing the greens. As you are likely aware, greens are an important part of every Black family's Thanksgiving dinner. So, to find the perfect bushel of greens, I took Mike to Nashville's Farmers' Market.[2] Our trip to the market was anything but a normal trip to the market. Mike spent about two hours carefully examining every bushel of greens on display that day. His greens selection process served as a reminder of the importance of paying attention to detail and of patience. He, in essence, was passing on the family's recipe of how to properly prepare greens for important family gatherings, and it started with selecting the perfect combination of collard greens and mustard greens. After our two-hour analysis of every bushel in the market, we went home to begin the two-day process of preparing greens for the family.

After we got home, we immediately soaked and washed the greens. Later that evening, we began the cooking process. We cooked them low and slow in an oven roaster capable of simmering overnight. The greens came out to perfection. While I already knew the importance of family, I was definitely reminded of that fact as a result of Mike's meticulous care for the family through his method of preparing greens.

Another occasion that was meaningful in my relationship with Mike was when we made the decision to move to Kansas City from Nashville. In celebration of completing my doctoral degree from Tennessee State University and to announce our planned departure from Nashville, we hosted a graduation/going away party. Because of the significance of the occasion, we invited a host of our friends and family from around the country. During the party, we carved out some time to thank our guests for attending and to officially announce that we were indeed leaving Nashville. I recall mentioning to the audience that I was a bit nervous about making the transition to Kansas City, as I was unfamiliar with the city and was worried about finding employment, and thus security for my family. As I was commenting about my trepidation, I remember hearing Mike yell from the back of the room with tears in his eyes, "don't worry son, we got your back."

He has definitely made good on his promise. After we arrived in Kansas City, he immediately began to help me become acquainted with the city. One of the ways that he chose to introduce me to the city was through attending the home games of his beloved Kansas City Chiefs. Admittedly, as a life-long Philadelphia Eagles fan, I wasn't expecting to fall in love with another team, but found myself slowly falling in love with the Chiefs. I now proudly tell my friends that I have two teams to cheer for in the National Football League. In the NFC, I of course have the Eagles, and in the AFC, I now have the Chiefs. It only becomes challenging when they are playing against each other, like in the 2025 Super Bowl. In games like that, win or lose, I still win.

My love for the Eagles can be traced back to my relationship with my father. He is a life-long Eagles fan and is responsible for introducing me to the Bird Gang. Likewise, my introduction to the Chiefs Kingdom can be traced back to my relationship with Mike. In the end, I am blessed to have Mike's fatherly presence in my life. In fact, I often say that not only has God blessed me with an amazing biological father, but was gracious enough to give me two additional fathers. I am truly fortunate to have three amazing fathers in my life.

My Father-Figures

I am also fortunate to have other father figures in my life who are of no biological relation but have contributed to my life in significant ways. Mr. Gary Maltbia is one such individual. In fact, he and his wife, Mrs. Anita Maltbia, have virtually adopted Stephenie and I as their surrogate children. They are our primary marriage counselors and coaches. We definitely have a stronger marriage because of their loving guidance and example.

Mr. Maltbia has also been my personal life coach and counselor. Interestingly, Mr. Maltbia is a former Employee Assistance Program (EAP) counselor and thus is quite easy to talk to. In fact, he is credited with founding the United Auto Workers EAP for General Motors CPC Division, Fairfax Assembly plant in Kansas City, KS.[3] Because of his skill level, coupled with his fatherly wisdom, he has a way of helping me address my problems without causing me to feel judged. He always makes time for me whenever I call. In consideration of his skill level and time rendered, I have often tried to compensate him monetarily, but to no avail. He never allows me to pay him, so from time to time, I will repay his generosity with his favorite bottle of Scotch.

He also fathers many of my peers throughout the city, so in this respect, I often refer to him as one of the fathers of Kansas City. I can truly say that not only am I a better person because of Mr. Maltbia's fatherly presence in my life, but Kansas City is a better city because of him.

Another father-figure in my life is Mr. James Scott. James and his wife Twana Scott (Mama T.), too, have adopted Stephenie and I as their surrogate children. They actually served as our realtors when we were house hunting fourteen years ago and have remained a significant part of our lives since that time. Like my father-in-law, Ullyses, I credit James with being a major part of helping us secure the home in which we have raised our family. In fact, the way in which we acquired our home is a rather fascinating story that James initiated. It's a story that I love telling.

On the day that we discovered our home, James and Mama T had scheduled several homes for us to visit. As we were exiting one of those homes, a gentleman that lived nearby approached us on the sidewalk and asked, "Are you all house hunting today? And if so, why aren't you interested in the house that I have for sale?" We replied, "we weren't aware that your home was for sale." The truth, however, was that we were aware that his house was for sale, but his home was out of our pre-determined price range.

After the gentleman's question, James immediately turned to us and instructed us to continue, with Mama T, to our next open house appointment and said that he would stay behind to chat with the gentleman who seemed to be eager to sell. We followed James' instructions and went to our next appointment, while he remained behind to investigate the gentleman's interest. After about twenty minutes or so, James rejoined us at the next appointment with the results of his conversation. He informed us that the gentleman's home was a "corporate sale." If you're like I was, you have no idea what a corporate sale is. Well, a corporate salc, also known as a relocation sale, involves a company assisting an employee with selling their home when they are relocating for work. This assistance can take various forms, including home marketing support, buying the home outright, or providing reimbursements for expenses. The goal is to make the relocation process as smooth as possible for the employee. It is also important to note that these kinds of arrangements often result in a streamlined sale that benefits both the seller and buyer.[4]

The gentleman had recently been relocated to another city for work and was eager to relocate his wife and three young children, who were still residing in Kansas City. His employer had already purchased the home on his behalf and was willing to sell at a reduced price in order to expedite the sale. James and Mama T masterfully assisted us throughout the process, with

James taking the lead on most of the negotiations that led to us acquiring our new home at a significantly reduced cost. In the end, we purchased our dream home within our pre-determined budget range, with instant equity to boot. I am forever grateful to James for his expert guidance.

Ultimately, it was James' keen awareness, business acumen and fatherly advice that led us to our dream home. And as mentioned above, our relationship with James and Mama T has persisted ever since. In fact, my relationship with James recently led to him asking me to serve as a pallbearer during his mother's funeral. It was one of the honors of my life to serve him and ultimately his mother in this way.

Another fun fact about my relationship with James is that we share a love for premium cigars and whiskey. I would not be exaggerating if I said that James is largely responsible for my new-found appreciation of good cigars paired with high quality whiskeys. I have become quite an aficionado because of James. 😉

Love Makes You a Father

Yet another outstanding father in my family is my brother-in-law, Troy. Troy's accomplishments as a father have been so impressive that this is not the first time that I have featured him in a publication that I have written. What has made him so impressive as a father is the fact that he has no biological children of his own. This aspect of Troy's fatherhood journey places him pretty high on my list of exceptional fathers. I often refer to him as *The Father* of his small village in Kansas City,

Kansas.

His journey into fatherhood started almost thirty years ago when he adopted my niece, Tiera, as his daughter. Tiera is my niece through marriage and is the biological daughter of my sister-in-law, Trina. Troy came into her life when she was a toddler and has been, for all intents and purposes, the only father she has ever known. He also serves as father to Lamonté, a young man that he and Trina have raised since birth. Lamonté is actually the biological son of a family friend who granted guardianship to Troy and Trina.

Fascinatingly, Troy is also the primary father-figure for his two grandchildren, who now live with him and Trina. Troy's grandchildren, "The Boys" as they are affectionately called throughout the family, recently moved in along with their mother, Tiera. While The Boys were certainly leading successful childhood lives prior to moving in with their grandparents, they are definitely thriving now that they have the everyday presence of their grandfather. Research has shown, which I will address in a subsequent chapter, that children do significantly better in several areas of their lives when there is a father-figure present in the household. Again, The Boys are doing quite well as a result of the consistent presence of their grandfather.[5]

Once again, Troy is one of the most impressive fathers that I know, largely because of his commitment to children who are, "supposedly", not his own. This truth causes me to recall a phrase that I have heard throughout my life, that "It is not flesh and blood, but heart which makes us fathers".[6] Troy is a glowing example of what lots of Black fathers have been doing for years, but unfortunately the narrative about Black fathers has been the complete opposite.

In the next chapter, I will introduce a number of my personal friends and acquaintances who are defying the stereotypes that are both said and believed about Black fathers in America. Many of these gentlemen lead extremely successful lives, with their accomplishments as fathers serving, arguably, as their most notable achievements. All of them have raised or are raising children who are leading successful lives. They are all glowing examples and, in many respects, representative of what and who Black fathers have been for decades in America.

The Responsibility and Reward of Young Fatherhood

Before I introduce my friends, there are a few additional fathers in my family that I must mention. First is my distant relative, Karlos. Karlos is a 23-year-old single father with sole custody of his one-year-old son. It would be a severe understatement to say that I am proud of him and am quite impressed with his willingness to take on this responsibility by himself. Sure, he has a strong village of supporters to assist him with his parenting duties, but it says a lot about him that he would step up and take sole responsibility for the upbringing of his son at this stage of his son's life.

At 23 years old, most young men are still navigating the tension between adolescence and adulthood. Most are barely making their own way, discovering their identity, and starting to find the rhythm of independence. This phase of life, for most, is a period of self-absorption and self-centeredness. It certainly was for me.

But for a young father like Karlos, with sole custody of his one-year-old son, life demands a kind of maturity that is shaped by a mixture of his own self-discovery, sacrifice, consistency, and uncertainty, joined with the quiet courage to be his son's primary example of manhood. From my vantage point, his fatherhood journey is in no way accidental. He is willingly choosing it day after day.

I am sure that his journey consists of early mornings wiping tears and more. I personally witnessed some of this a few months ago, when we last spent some time with him and his son, Koda. I saw him, first-hand, balancing diaper changes with nap time, and making decisions that placed his son's well-being before his own. In a society that often questions the commitment of young fathers, especially young African American fathers, his commitment defies stereotypes and reclaims a profound truth. He is determined not to be a footnote in his son's story, hc is actively writing its earliest chapters.

The significance of his presence is much greater than the daily tasks that he performs, they will manifest in the person his son will become in the future. He is his son's primary protector, provider and nurturer, which is very much aligned with what most of the fathers in his family have done before him. His youth does not diminish his capacity to do and be these things, in many ways, it amplifies the energy required to grow alongside his son. Where others may see limitations because of his youth, I see possibilities.

Again, I am extremely impressed with, not just his courage, but his dogged determination and devotion. Without overstating it, I believe that this young father's journey is quite inspiring. It challenges cultural myths, redefines masculinity, and plants seeds of generational transformation. His son will not only know his father's name, but he will also know his father's love, his father's sacrifice, and his father's abundant presence. And in that lies the making of a powerful legacy, not just for his son, but for all others who are watching.

Love Endures Beyond Physical Boundaries

Incarceration often casts a long shadow of disruption and discord over families. It often results in severed family ties, sometimes broken forever. Miraculously, some families are able to weather the storm that incarceration often creates. Even more remarkably, some incarcerated fathers manage to maintain authentic connections with their children from behind bars. My brother, Eric, is one such father. Incredibly, he has maintained fruitful relationships with his children, though incarcerated.

He is the first to admit that he is the sole person responsible for the chasm that exists between him and his children. He also takes ownership of the fact that he has not always done things right regarding his relationships with his children. Still, the strong connection that he has maintained with his kids is a testament, not only to a love that endures beyond physical boundaries, but also to the legacy that our dad has passed on. Proverbs 13:22 says that "a good man leaves an inheritance for his children's children".[7] Along with the authentic bonds that my brother has obviously established with his children, he is also reaping the blessings that our dad has sown.

First and foremost, my brother's connections with his children cannot be measured by proximity, but by intentionality. He has, over the years, written letters, made phone calls when he can, and has found ways to remain emotionally attached to his children. His children know his voice as well as his unwavering belief in their potential. He has worked hard not to define himself by his circumstances, but instead has chosen to define himself as a caring family member and a devoted father.

The significance of his presence is, in many ways, palpable. It challenges the narrative that incarceration must translate into separation or abandonment. It actually affirms that intention, when rooted in love, can stretch across distance and circumstances. His commitment has become a lifeline, not just for his children, but for himself. In nurturing and supporting his kids, he reclaims his humanity.

It goes without saying that his fatherhood story is not one of perfection, but it certainly is one of perseverance and resolve. It is a reminder that presence is not always physical, it can manifest through emotional and spiritual ties, if there's intentionality. I truly believe that in the hearts of his children, he is not a man behind bars. He is a source of strength, a voice of guidance, and a symbol of enduring love.

CHAPTER THREE

MY FRIENDS ARE GREAT FATHERS

"Fathers, the call is clear: Our presence is the ultimate present."
Jason Wilson

Undeniably, one of the most damaging misnomers about Black fathers, and thus the Black community, is the myth of the "absent Black father". Recent research and its resultant findings prove that Black fathers are not absent and have actually been more active in their children's lives than fathers from other ethnic groups.[1] *I will discuss these research data in a subsequent chapter.* In this chapter, I will highlight men who are "real life" examples of the aforementioned data. A good number of these men are my personal friends and acquaintances. All of them are outstanding fathers.

Although several scholars and research groups have recently studied African American fathers, there is much more to learn about this segment of our country's citizenry. Unfortunately, Black fathers have, largely, been marginalized and thus overlooked, especially with regard to our good deeds and achievements. Our marginalization has led to gross misinterpretations of who we are, and in many cases, blatant lies are being told about us. As a member of this group, I have vowed to help tell the truth about who we are and have been for our families and communities for a very long time.

Because I personally know the gentlemen who are featured in this chapter and share similar backgrounds, experiences and identity with them, I chose individual interviews as well as group interviews to gather their insights. This heuristic approach to information collection allowed me to maintain my identity as part of the group and not just a mere observer or outgroup data collector. It is important to mention that our conversations required a level of vulnerability that's not exactly customary in men. Our discussions were intimate, heart-felt, and honest. They provided tangible insights into what fatherhood looks and feels like, specifically, from the African American perspective. Again, my method of information gathering was up-close and personal, which fostered authentic and genuine dialogue. It is also important to mention that during the group interviews, I participated in the discussions and moderated in such a way to encourage the fathers to respond to each other's comments. This provided for a rich exchange of thoughts, ideas and feelings.

From our conversations, there emerged seven themes/ principles that capture the essence of fatherhood. Of course, there were dozens of themes, but these seven were most prominent and recurring. The list below reveals the emergent themes along with corresponding narratives that attempt to define and/or describe the principle:

THEME/PRINCIPLE	DEFINITION/DESCRIPTION
PRESENCE	EACH FATHER EXPRESSED THE IMPORTANCE OF HAVING A CONSIST PRESENCE IN THEIR CHILDREN'S LIVES.
PROTECTION	PROVIDING PHYSICAL, EMOTIONAL AND PSYCHOLOGICAL SAFETY IS A MAJOR COMPONENT OF FATHERHOOD.

ADVOCACY	THROUGHOUT LIFE, OUR CHILDREN WILL NEED US TO SPEAK UP FOR THEM.
SACRIFICE	FATHERHOOD REQUIRES SELFLESSNESS.
RESPONSIBILITY	FATHERHOOD NECESSITATES AN UNDERSTANDING THAT YOU ARE RESPONSIBLE FOR MORE THAN JUST YOURSELF.
PERSONHOOD	THEY WON'T KNOW WHO THEY ARE IF THEY DON'T KNOW YOU.
PERSEVERANCE	NEVER GIVE UP.

The men highlighted here are a cross-section of Black Fatherhood in America. A few of them would be classified as "single" fathers as they have sole custody of their children, some de jure and others de facto, and thus are extremely active in their children's lives. Others are fathers as well as husbands, and parent their children alongside their wives and are fully engaged in the comings and goings of their children's daily activities. Interestingly, the fathers who now have adult children still play a significant role in their adult children's lives. As a result, their children are now leading very successful adult lives. Below are the results of our conversations:

Presence

The theme, *Presence*, is one of the most prominent of all the themes that arose from our conversations. Each father, at some point, mentioned *presence* as an important component of fatherhood. A father's presence, both physically and emotionally, is critical to a child's social development and provides for a healthy sense of self. As I alluded to earlier when talking about my own successes in relationship to my father's ubiquitous presence in my life, our children develop a strong sense of self and security when we fathers are consistently present in their lives. Children learn how to regulate their emotions as a result of consistent and responsive care from parents, with fathers playing a unique role in helping children to feel safe to explore the world.[2]

This point causes me to recall that when our children were young, my wife and I would intentionally allow them to roam freely and explore their surroundings when we were out in public spaces. It was one of my daughter's favorite things to do when she was a toddler. In fact, it became one of our bonding rituals as father and daughter. Our public space of choice was Opry Mills Mall in Nashville, Tennessee. It is a one level, 1.2 million square foot structure with a racetrack style floor plan. One lap around the mall is equivalent to 1 mile.[3]

On a regular basis, my daughter and I would venture out to the mall, mainly, for recreation and exercise. I would often allow her to trot approximately 30 to 40 feet in front of me as we made our laps around the mall. Throughout our laps, she would turn around to make sure that she could see me and I could see her. I would give her a reassuring wave and smile that I was, indeed, still there and that she was free and safe to continue her exploration. I believe these kinds of moments created in her the confidence and courage to venture one thousand miles away from home after high school to attend her dream school in Washington, DC, Howard University. I'm witnessing the same confidence and courage in my son who is concluding his freshman year, eight hundred miles away from home in the Southeastern region of the country.

I realize that these kinds of accomplishments are relatively common, but I would encourage you to refrain from underestimating the substance that fuels them. I believe that one of the ingredients that fuels these kinds of achievements is the presence of a caring and responsive parent or adult. If you're thinking that mothers have been serving in these roles too, then you're absolutely correct. Of course, mothers have been universally present in their children's lives. In concert with a mother's presence, I believe that a present father contributes to a child's emotional stability, security, and resilience in ways that are different, but complementary to a mother's presence. A father often models a different range of emotional expressions that helps children develop a strong sense of self and confidence.

When interviewing the fathers, I asked a series of questions related to their overall philosophy and experiences as fathers. One of the questions intently asked, *"What is the best decision you have ever made as a father?"*. Kansas City, Missouri Businessman/entrepreneur, high school baseball coach and father of three, C. Evans. said the following:

> *"Showing up for my kids every day, is one of the best decisions I have ever made as a father."*

Relatedly, when asked, *"What advice would you give to young fathers?"* Evans emphatically stated that young fathers should:

> *"Stop whatever you're doing and be present in your kids' lives, especially, when they really need you."*

Again, as I have alluded to throughout this book, I believe that our children become who they are as a result of the time they spend with us. Relatedly, another question that I asked fathers was: *"What traditions did your father pass on to you that you have now passed on to your children?"* If I were to answer my own question here, I would say that my father passed on the tradition of "consistently spending time with my children".

I trust that you recall me mentioning, in Chapter 1, that one of the ways that my dad chose to spend time with us was through coaching our Pop Warner football teams when we were kids. Well, I did a very similar thing with my children. I coached my son's baseball teams from the time he was 6 years old until he was 13 years old. I also would serve as a substitute coach, from time to time, for my daughter's soccer team when she was young. The interesting thing was, I really didn't consciously decide to coach their teams, it kind of just happened organically. I guess it was implanted in my subconscious mind as a result of seeing my father coach us years ago.

(Funny Note: At my wife's advice, I intentionally chose not to serve as the permanent coach for my daughter's soccer teams and later her volleyball teams, because we surmised that my intense style of coaching would have scared a group of 7-year-old little girls. 😊)

Protection

Being the family's *"Protector"* is the role most associated with fatherhood. It is often assumed that physical safety is the only form of *protection* that's expected and thus required of fathers. The truth is *protection* goes beyond physical safety. Fatherhood is about providing security, guidance, and unwavering support throughout a child's life. *Protection* ultimately includes emotional safety as well as psychological safety. In this regard, *protection* is a natural companion to the previous principle, *presence*, as *protection* facilitates the confidence and courage that *presence* initiates. In other words, protection is the backdrop to presence. Our presence as fathers often translates into protection.

As a case in point, in the scenario described above, where I allowed my daughter to trot several feet in front of me during our trips to the mall, my presence indicated that she was safe; that she had protection as she explored her surroundings. Protection invoked psychological safety in that my daughter not only felt safe, but she cognitively understood that she was safe as a result of confirming that I was still walking behind her. This is why I have often compared a father's leadership to that of a shepherd. Shepherds typically lead from behind their flock. While a shepherd may, from time to time, move to the front to scout for danger or to guide the flock in a specific direction, a shepherd's primary role is to monitor, nurture and protect the sheep from the rear. From behind, the shepherd allows the stronger, more agile sheep to set the pace for the flock.[4] In many respects, this scenario is analogous to helping our eldest children attain high achievements, which optimistically will cause younger children to follow suit.

Father of four and long-time Kansas City, Missouri youth basketball coach, T. Taylor gives commentary to this very concept:

> *"I told my kids, I don't accept C's in my house....and your oldest child is the key to the standards you set. If you get your oldest child on the right path, everyone else falls into place. So, in my house, grades weren't negotiable. C's are*

average and average is not acceptable. I only accept A's and B's in my house."

Taylor now has four adult children who are leading very successful lives. His oldest child is now in law school after successfully earning a bachelor's degree while also competing as a Division I basketball player. His second oldest child is an up-and-coming businessman in the Kansas City community, and he too recently obtained a bachelor's degree while competing as a Division I basketball player. His daughters, the Twins, recently earned their undergraduate degrees and are both now pursuing graduate degrees in the medical industry.

It appears that the "No C's" standard that Taylor set for his children worked. Again, they all are now leading successful lives because of the great parenting of Taylor and his wife, Mrs. Taylor. But, because this book is dedicated to great fathers, I'm placing special emphasis on the parenting of Mr. Taylor.

Relatedly, I recall a funny story that took place several years ago, involving my children, that mirrors what has been illustrated by the Taylors. During a parent-teacher conference with my son's first grade teacher, she shared that after completing a test one day, my son asked her to grade his test immediately. When she asked him why there was such urgency in grading his test, he stated that he wanted to make sure that he was getting good grades just like his big sister.

While this is an endearing story about a, then, six-year-old kid aspiring to make good grades like an older sibling, nestled in this story are the high expectations that were set for an older sibling, which had trickled down to the younger sibling. The high expectations were established by a flourishing household, consisting of an engaged mother and an involved father.

Interestingly, research has linked academic success to the involvement of fathers specifically. [5] Often, the involvement simply translates into a father being an advocate for his child. So, again, the stories above have a lot to do with a father's presence and the protection that he provides, but woven into the stories, too, is a healthy measure of advocacy. This leads us to the next principle/theme:

Advocacy

Fathers who actively support and speak up for their children contribute to their children's development in profound ways. Research shows that involved fathers help boost a child's social intelligence, emotional regulation, and academic performance. [6] When a dad champions his child's needs, whether in school, in social settings or elsewhere, it builds a child's sense of certainty and well-being. When a father steps up to *advocate* for his child, it sends a powerful message, not just to the outside world, but to the child him or herself. It tells a child that "You matter." Your voice matters and your father has your back.

Kansas City, Missouri Businessman/Entrepreneur and father of three, D. Piggie, highlights this point, even when advocating for a child among family members. Below he talks about a scenario where he spoke up on his daughter's behalf to his daughter's mother.

> *"Just today, I was coordinating the payment of my daughter's soccer, track & field, and basketball fees with*

> *her mother and mentioned that Denver [our daughter] really didn't want to play soccer but was simply playing because she [her mother] wanted her to play. She was only playing to make her mother happy."*

As suggested here, advocacy is not just about social or academic outcomes, it can deepen the father-child bond. A father's advocacy shows a child what love in action looks like. Like in an earlier part of this book, where I described an instance where my dad advocated for, not just me, but for my entire high school football team, in so doing, he served as a model for standing up for what is right. In that scenario, he taught us how to advocate for ourselves and for others.

And also, as implied above, advocacy does not always happen in big ripples or has major consequences. Sometimes, it's a simple gesture like described above where a dad is indirectly helping a child find her voice. However, advocacy in school or educational settings can be extremely effective when done correctly. T. Taylor shares commentary below that underlines the importance of advocating for our children in educational settings:

> *"When my kids first started school, I made it a practice to never openly disagree or argue with their teachers. I made sure that they understood that their teachers and I were on the same team, that they were to follow the instructions of their teachers, that their teachers were an extension of their mom and me...however, there was one situation where a teacher issued a Friday deadline for a group project and when one student from the group turned in their assignment early on Wednesday, he then gave the rest of*

> *the group zeroes. I immediately called a meeting with him to advocate for all of the kids, because it appeared that he had moved the goalpost."*

Congruently, advocacy does not always require vocal or verbal intervention. At times, advocacy simply requires your presence as a parent. For instance, in school settings, I believe that teachers and administrators will treat your children according to the amount of advocacy they have from a parent or guardian. I am not suggesting that teachers and administrators are intentionally malicious toward students who don't have parents who are present, I am simply suggesting that teachers and administrators do better when they know that a parent or guardian is there to hold them accountable. This point is made in the commentary below, where long-time Kansas City, Missouri high school football and track & field coach, entrepreneur and single father of three, A. Wilson, simply showed up to have lunch with his son:

> *"When my son was in middle school, I remember a situation where he was having some challenges with one of his teachers. I didn't want to wait until the parent-teacher conference to address the issue, so I decided to simply go have lunch with my son, just to make my presence known. As I was sitting there with my son, several teachers stopped by our table and asked, "is there anything wrong or is there anything that we can help you with" ....it turned out that I never really had to address the issue, directly. The challenges with the teacher just went away."*

Mr. Wilson's commentary triggers my recollection of a situation that my family and I dealt with when my daughter was in elementary school. One afternoon, we received an unexpected phone call from our daughter's principal requesting our presence at an impromptu meeting. She informed us that our daughter had gotten into a minor misunderstanding with a teacher and that the teacher, when recounting the incident, described our daughter as a "little ghetto girl". Her use of the expression "little ghetto girl" was, of course, intended to be harmful. The teacher wasn't our daughter's regular classroom instructor but served as the school's Art instructor. Our daughter's principal went on to say that she simply wanted the teacher to "see us" and anticipated that the misunderstanding would resolve itself with a brief meeting.

We accepted her invitation and agreed to meet her and the teacher the very next day during the morning drop-off period. When I walked into the front entrance of the school, the principal warmly greeted me by saying, "Good Morning, Dr. Smith" with a big smile on her face. In an adjacent room, I could see the teacher overhearing the principal as she greeted me. The teacher's head dropped immediately, seemingly in regret and sorrow. My wife entered the building a few minutes later, receiving the same warm greeting from the principal.

I honestly don't remember much about the meeting, however, I do remember that I didn't say much during the meeting. Interestingly, most of the meeting didn't really address the misunderstanding. The meeting mainly consisted of my wife and the principal discussing some of the community work that my wife and I were engaged in at the time, and the teacher largely sat in silence. After the meeting, we never received another call concerning that teacher or the misunderstanding. I believe that our daughter's principal simply wanted the teacher to "see us" and gain an understanding that Phoenix wasn't a "little ghetto girl." I presume that our presence, alone, served as confirmation of that fact.

Other examples of advocacy sometimes involve a parent, in this case, a father speaking on behalf of a child to the parent of another child. In the scenario below, Kansas City, Missouri Salesman and father of two adult children, B. Jackson, Sr., describes a situation where his daughter was in somewhat of a "character dispute" with the son of a childhood friend. Below, Mr. Jackson describes an exchange that took place with his childhood friend regarding their children's dispute.

> *"I've spent the past 14 years raising my daughter to be a lady… to be protective of her reputation as a lady. And because I know you and know how you were raised, I know that you've raised your son to be honest and be a man of integrity…my daughter has provided me with evidence that your son is spreading lies about her at school. I would really appreciate it if you would advise him to stop doing that."*

(Mr. Jackson asked me to share this "sanitized" version of the exchange, as the actual exchange was a bit more expressive. 😊)

In the end, advocacy can shape a child's life far more meaningfully than most of us realize. It's not just about speaking up for our kids. It's about creating the conditions in which a child learns who they are and what they should believe about themselves, often guiding how they move through the world. Advocacy shields children from harm, physically, emotionally, and socially. When adults intervene, challenge unfairness, or ensure that a child's needs are met, that child learns the she or he deserves safety and care.

Advocacy models what it looks like to speak truth, to ask questions, and challenge status quo. Children don't start out with fully formed voices. Over time, they internalize the examples led by the adults in their lives and begin advocating for themselves and others as a result. Seeing advocacy in action teaches children that systems can be navigated, challenged and changed. It builds a sense of agency in our children.

Children who grow up with strong advocates in their lives often develop internal narratives about themselves and others that are far different than children who are forced to navigate the world alone. Advocacy plants seeds of empathy and leadership, skills that will echo into adulthood. They learn what matters, often with those beliefs serving as the foundation for everything else they build in life.

Sacrifice

A father's *sacrifice* can be one of the most profound and powerful forms of love given. It might show up in small, subtle ways, like a missed opportunity at work in order to be home more often, sleepless nights worrying about college tuition, or letting go of personal aspirations so a child or children can chase theirs. And sometimes, it's bigger than that, like working multiple jobs, moving your family across town or to another state for a better life, or standing firm in tough choices that won't win praise but are made out of care. The impact of those sacrifices often unfold over time. Children may not always notice in the moment, but later in life, they often look back and understand the magnitude of what was given. It shapes their values, reinforces their understanding of love, and often inspires them to pay those gifts forward.

My lifelong friend, father of two young adult children and Charlotte, North Carolina entrepreneur, J.L. White, talks about this very thing in the comments below. When asked, *"What kind of relationship do you have with your father?"*, White said the following:

> *"Considering the things that I know now as a father, I appreciate my father even more for the things I know that he had to sacrifice, for the things he had to deal with and for the things he had to navigate….and to still be, not just present, but extremely active in my life through all of it. I now have something I can measure it by because I am now in the same position…I now look back in amazement of what he did, and it actually causes my relationship with him to be even more special."*

Again, sacrifice is often the invisible backbone of fatherhood, it doesn't always make the headlines but is felt in every aspect of a child's life. A father's willingness to put his children's needs above his own can manifest through choosing to be present, even when life demands otherwise. It endures hardship, financial, emotional and otherwise, so that the family doesn't have to. It teaches lessons not always with lectures, but with actions and humility. And as mentioned before, it manifests in fathers setting aside their own personal aspirations to ensure their children can chase theirs. These sacrifices aren't about grand gestures, they are often woven into everyday life and become a father's new goals and dreams. This is the essence of the remarks offered by my dear friend, Atlanta, Georgia entrepreneur and father of four, T.L. Dixon. He answered the question, *"What advice would you give to young fathers?"* in the following way:

> *"Once you learn how to surrender yourself to your children's needs, those obligations become your joy. You will then begin to build everything around your parenting. Before that, you may have been focused solely on your lifestyle and your various personal enjoyments. But when your parenting becomes your enjoyment, from my vantage point, life becomes a lot easier.... you've got to mentally and emotionally surrender yourself to your family. Tell yourself that this is just what we do as fathers."*

In the end, sacrifice is a defining thread in the fabric of fatherhood. A father's love is rarely loud. It doesn't always announce itself with grand gestures or poetic words. More often, it moves in silence, felt in the sacrifices made without fanfare, in the choices that put others first. Father of four, T. Taylor, says the following with regard to sacrifice:

> *"If you're not willing to sacrifice, fatherhood is not possible.... you have to embrace the sacrifice of fatherhood....you will be miserable, if you don't fully understand and embrace your responsibilities as a father...I've spent $100K in tuition the last four years...I'm still driving my old car, I'm not making many changes on the house right now because of my commitment to my kids."*

My lifelong friend, Georgetown, South Carolina Music Producer, and father of three young adult children, G. Nesbit, perfectly articulates the power and significance of a father's sacrifice:

> *"God sacrificing Jesus can be seen as a mirror of the sacrifice [fathers] make for their children. Just as God gave what was most precious so that others might live, [fathers] give of themselves daily…time, energy, comfort, and even parts of their dreams, so their children can have a future. The metaphor teaches that true love is not measured by what we keep, but by what we are willing to give way for those we love most."*

To be a father is to give without keeping score. It is passing on the last piece of chicken and eating what's left after your family has eaten. It is staying until the last out is called on the baseball diamond and getting up at the crack of dawn the next morning to do it all over again. It is exchanging personal aspirations for responsibilities and doing so without regret because in your children's accomplishments you find your joy. It is the long drives to baseball, football, basketball, soccer, or volleyball tournaments. It is earnest prayers and silent endurance. It is standing tall through life's storms so your family can rest in peace and certainty. And in all these ways, sacrifice becomes your language of love. So, to all the fathers, past, present, and those to come, who carry their families, not just on your backs, but in your hearts, your strength is not forgotten. Your quiet devotion echoes across generations. Your dedication is in honor of what our enslaved ancestors were forced to endure when they were snatched away from their families. So, as in the greeting offered to each other by our Zulu brothers and sisters of South Africa, I say to you "Sawubona!"

Responsibility

Responsibility is one of the cornerstones of fatherhood. It is not just a duty, but a calling, a deep and on-going commitment. When a man becomes a father, he steps into a role that demands his undivided attention, his deepest veracity, joined with stubborn fortitude. Fatherhood, when honored to its strictest fidelity, does not come with an on/off switch. It is, rather, a full-time, all day, everyday commitment. A father's responsibility means being there from the first breath through every stage of life, providing stability, security, guidance, and support, even when it's inconvenient, difficult or thankless.

In, perhaps, the group interview that inspired most of this chapter, retired US Army Lieutenant Colonel and Kansas City, Missouri Businessman/Entrepreneur and father of five, G. Bryant, said the following about the responsibility of fatherhood. His commentary was specifically in response to the following question, *"What do you remember about the birth of each of your children?*

> *"For my first child, I had just bought a 1991 Ford Probe, mainly, because that's all I could afford at the time. The truth is, I really couldn't afford it, but I needed a family car, because prior to that, I had a truck, which wasn't appropriate for the baby's car seat. I remember putting my son in the car and the entire ride back to our apartment, I was just worried about how I was gonna feed my family.... How am I gonna do this? Because it's not just me and my wife anymore, we have another mouth to feed.... Am I a man now, if so, what do I do? How do I persevere?"*

Bryant's commentary calls to mind a conversation

that I had with a mentor years ago. During this particular conversation, I asked my mentor to define maturity. Her response was quite profound and thought-provoking. She defined maturity as "having the desire to be responsible for another life." When I first heard her definition, I pushed back, using the self-protective logic that parenthood should not be the only way to reach maturity. She replied that her definition did not specifically name parenthood as a requirement, though it could be insinuated. It simply emphasized responsibility for another life, which could be a sibling, an aging parent, a spouse or even a pet. Maturity doesn't necessarily translate into parenthood, but it definitely is required in order to be a parent.

When we really think about it, my mentor's definition of maturity actually invokes a better understanding of citizenship. When we come to the realization that we are responsible for more than just ourselves, we become better citizens. Her definition not only invokes a sense of responsibility, but also a sense of community.

Later in the aforementioned group interview, G. Bryant offered a similar definition of maturity. He asserts that "maturity is understanding that you are no longer the most important person in your life." His definition, too, does not explicitly name parenthood as a requirement, but it, too, insinuates it. Thus, I have over the years, argued that parenthood, and especially fatherhood, helps men to grow up, expressly if and when maturity has been delayed in any way. Ultimately, as a father, the sooner you gain an understanding that you are no longer the most important person in your life, the better off you and your family will be. Fatherhood necessitates an understanding that you are, forever, responsible for more than just yourself. Therefore, it can be said that fatherhood not only creates better men, but better homes, which spawns better communities, cities, states, countries and ultimately, a better world.

During the same group interview, single father of two young adult children and Kansas City, Missouri Computer Scientist, R. Thomas, said the following about is children:

> *"I always tell people that my daughter saved my life, and my son changed my life…before them I was in the streets doing stupid (expletive) but having them made me responsible for something bigger than myself."*

And perhaps, most importantly, our children learn from witnessing a father's adherence to his responsibilities. A responsible father models accountability, patience, and moral courage to do the right thing even if it's unfamiliar or uncomfortable. A father is a living example of the kind of adult he hopes his children will grow to be. Even when the world demands more of a father's time, a responsible father carves out time for his children, showing them through consistent action that they are valued.

My lifelong friend, J.L. White, offers commentary about this very thing when talking about his father's on-going commitment when we were young:

> *"I really don't know how he did it. He was always there, even when I wasn't expecting him to be. Like when we played high school football, I'm sure there were games that my dad missed, but I simply can't remember any that he missed…. I even remember him showing up at games*

where he was supposed to have been at work."

Remarkably, I remember many of the instances that J.L. White describes above. My dad and his dad actually worked together and would often slip away from their duties at work to attend our high school football games. They were both employed at the steel mill mentioned in Chapter 1, which was literally one block away from our high school football stadium.

Again, a major part of fatherhood means showing up for your children even when they don't expect you to. It lets them know that they are valued. It also gives them "real life" examples of what they should do, if and when they become parents.

In the end, responsibility is more than a trait of fatherhood, it is in many respects the very heartbeat of it. When all is said and done, a father's sense of responsibility reaches far beyond paying bills or meeting daily needs. It is an enduring, often an unspoken promise to provide, to protect, and to guide. It is a constant effort to lay a foundation on which his children can safely build their lives.

From the moment a man becomes a father, something at his fundamental core shifts. His choices begin to reflect a deeper purpose, no longer centered on himself, but on the small lives that now depend on him. Whether he is driving his newborn child home for the first time or helping a teenager navigate the throes of adolescence, the weight of his role never leaves his shoulders. And for most fathers, responsibility is carried, not with complaint, but with quiet determination.

Responsible fathers understand that their presence matters. They know that showing up for recitals or basketball games has a lasting impact. But perhaps what makes a father's responsibility most profound is that it is not driven only by obligation, but by love. It is not always glamorous or noticed, and rarely does it seek praise. Yet, it is through this sense of purpose that fathers shape generations. This sentiment is captured in the commentary below offered by, R. Thomas:

> *"When I was a kid playing basketball, when I got up of the bench to go in the game, my dad was the one person I would be looking for in the crowd, and he was always there."*

In a society that often overlooks these quiet providers, fathers who shoulder responsibility with humility and strength deserve to be honored. Their steady presence anchors their families, their decisions protect their families' future, and their unwavering dedication leaves imprints not just on their children, but on the world their children will one day influence.

Personhood

Fathers generate *personhood* in their children. Our offspring find out who they are as a result of the time they spend with us. I have often said that "our children will be who they see." From a child's earliest days, a father's presence evokes a kind of invisible architecture, providing a foundation, structure, and protection. A father doesn't necessarily define the child, but he offers a mirror, not to clone, but to reflect. An affirming smile, a loving word of correction, the way he carries his burdens with grace, these become emotional guideposts that steer a child's internal compass.

A father's presence offers more than proximity, it is a steady rhythm in the background of a child's becoming. Not always loud, not always perfect, but deeply formative. A father's presence marks the beginning of a child's journey toward discovering their own identity, not through imposition, but through subtle, and not so subtle, lessons of wisdom and direction.

Below, my lifelong friend, G. Nesbit, succinctly and profoundly articulates the importance of a father's presence and guidance:

> *"For most of human history, the family, elders, teachers, and local community were the main 'libraries' young people had. Information was filtered through experience, culture, and relationships. Now, with Google, YouTube, TikTok, and A.I., the flow of information bypasses traditional authority figures entirely. Kids can instantly access answers and competing perspectives, often from strangers who speak with confidence (whether they're right or not). That shift changes the parent/child dynamic. It's not that youth don't need guidance, they still desperately do, but the role of a [father] is no longer just being a 'source of facts'. It's about being a guide through the noise.*
>
> *The paradox is that even though the internet has made knowledge free, wisdom is now more valuable than ever, and wisdom still comes best from trusted human connection. Facts can be searched. Wisdom must be lived. [Fathers] must be the example they can't Google."*

Very much in alignment with the above quote, Kansas City, Missouri Jazz Musician and father of two, E. Freeman,

Jr. says the following regarding his identity as it relates to his father's guidance and presence in his life:

> *"Looking back at my life, I realize more than ever, that I am my father's son. In a lot of ways, I recognize that I am a carbon copy of my father, mainly because of the quality time I spent with him as a kid."*

As children grow, they begin to untangle themselves from their father's shadow, testing boundaries, asking questions, and in many cases, pushing limits. But the presence of a father, consistently showing up, being emotionally available, guiding from a healthy distance, creates the safety that makes their self-exploration possible. A father's belief in who they can become sow seeds of confidence, even when they can't yet see it for themselves.

It is in this tension between dependence and autonomy, between heritage and individuality that identity is formed. A child begins to realize *I am not my father, but I carry pieces of him with me.* The way I speak with conviction. The way I sit with silence. The courage to stand up for what I believe in. Through him, I inherited more than physical features or a last name, I inherited the framework to build a life that is uniquely mine.

G. Bryant, when talking about the impact that a father can have on his children's lives, offered the following words:

> *"The magnitude in which you can affect your children's lives, can't really be measured…In a conversation with my son recently, he said that he was really thankful to have me in his life…He was reflecting on a conversation that he*

> *had had with a group of his co-workers who were talking about the fact that their fathers weren't a part of their lives…he called to thank me that that wasn't his story. He was thankful that there was never a time that I wasn't there for him."*

Fathers who are present, physically, emotionally, and spiritually give their children not just direction, but permission. Permission to explore. Permission to feel. Permission to become. Their presence is the unspoken force that says: *You are not alone in your becoming.* And one day, when the child grows into adulthood, and looks in the mirror, they may not see their father's face staring back at them, but they will see the imprint of his love and wisdom woven into their own life. Not as a map, but as a compass. Not as a destiny, but as a launching pad. A father's presence, then, is not just about shaping who his children are, it is about offering a solid foundation so they can discover who they are meant to be, authentically.

This thought, interestingly enough, causes me to recall the story of my paternal grandfather, Abraham "Pickett" Fraser. I, unfortunately, never had the pleasure of meeting my grandfather. He died on Christmas Day of the year I was born, 1971. You may recall that I was born in Philadelphia and thus, my grandfather didn't have the chance to meet me in my first six months of life because he lived in Georgetown, South Carolina. My parents told me that we traveled back down to Georgetown to celebrate Christmas with our family and I was actually on my way to meet my grandfather for the first time, when he unexpectantly died.

During my youth, I would frequently ask my dad to show

me a picture of my grandfather, but unfortunately, he did not have a photo of him. In place of a picture, my dad would encourage me to go look in the mirror, because according to family folklore, I resemble him a lot. Over the years, I have come to believe that not only do I resemble him, physically, but I also resemble his fundamental essence. I say this because, if I am a reflection of my father and my father a reflection of my grandfather, then I, too, am a reflection of my grandfather. I also say this because my parents shared that when they got married back in 1963, my grandfather gave them seven thousand dollars as a wedding gift. If you're wondering what the purchasing power of seven thousand dollars was in 1963 in comparison to today's purchasing power, it is equivalent to roughly seventy-four thousand dollars in 2026.

Here's my point: I realize that money alone does not equate to being a great father. However, I believe my grandfather truly loved his son (my father) and provided my mom and dad with a great launching pad for their marriage, and thus a great foundation for my brother and me to be raised. And to be more straightforward, part of the reason why my dad could never produce a photo of his father was because he did not have much of a relationship with his father, at least, not until he was an adult. This point leads us to the final principle of fatherhood. It appears that my grandfather never gave up on building a meaningful relationship with his son. Fatherhood requires all of the previously mentioned principles and culminates with the notion that fatherhood often requires perseverance.

Perseverance

Fatherhood is not a role that is earned once and worn forever like an Olympic medal. It is a daily choice, a lifelong test, and a living commitment that demands *perseverance.* Fatherhood is a promise kept, in perpetuity. It is forged in both the extraordinary moments and the ordinary days, in the subtle sacrifices, and in the countless times a father shows up despite having his own challenges or even fears. While love is the ingredient that ignites the spirit of fatherhood, it is perseverance that sustains it.

Perseverance in fatherhood is often unspoken and in a lot of ways undetectable to the untrained eye. It is the father who stays up after working the late shift to help with homework. It is the father who grapples with the weight of providing, guiding, and protecting, even when his own footing is uncertain. These everyday acts, repeated faithfully without applause, are often what define great fathers. They persist not because it's easy, but because their children's needs refuse to wait for perfect conditions.

For some, fatherhood collides with competing pressures, often interrupted by strained or fractured relationships, self-doubt or uncertainty as well as the pervasiveness of scarce resources. In these valleys, perseverance becomes more than endurance, it transforms into tenacity. It is the refusal to abandon your post, to remain present even when you feel empty and depleted. True fatherhood, then, is less about perfection and more about persistence.

Local Kansas City, Missouri Entrepreneur and single father of three young adult children, E. Brown, talks about the challenges of parenting while living in a different state than a child.

> *"I have not always gotten it right when it comes to my kids, especially with my daughter, who lives in another state…I am really proud of the progress we've made though…we talk more now than ever before, and I believe it is because I never gave up on having a relationship with her, despite the challenges I have had with her mother. I am proud to say that I persevered."*

While this book is exclusively focused on the nuances of fatherhood, a lot of the interviewees are also husbands. And thus, a percentage of our dialogue drifted between two identities, father and husband, each sacred, each demanding, and sometimes each pulling in different directions. These roles, while deeply fulfilling, are also layered with complexity. They require a man to live in dual devotion, nurturing his children while honoring the covenant of marriage. In a world that often celebrates independence and self-fulfillment, choosing the path of committed love and fatherhood demands a special balance of resilience, humility, and determination.

Kansas City, Missouri Salesman and father of three children, J. Madge captures a glimpse of what life is like for men who actively serve in both roles:

> *"Being a husband and father is a twenty-five hours a day, 8 days a week job…you gotta make sure everybody is O.K…your wife, your kids and everything else. And a lot of times there's very little gratitude…guys who serve as dads and husbands speak a peculiar language."*

While both roles require perseverance, fatherhood demands a dynamic set of approaches in order to be successful. Our children often require a kind of nuanced approach. They grow, but they grow in different areas of their lives at different paces. For instance, emotional maturity may not grow as quickly as physical maturity. They often make mistakes and push boundaries that fathers must respond to with grace, patience and leniency. Perseverance in this context means choosing to teach rather than punish, to listen instead of lecture, and to stay engaged when it would be easier to detach. A father's influence is cumulative, it's not always achieved in broad strokes but in repeated acts of stability and consistency. J. Madge calls to attention the importance of consistency when nurturing your children:

> *"If there's a secret sauce to fatherhood…if I had to sum it up in one word, it would be consistency…keep showing up…To help your kids become productive adults, you have to model consistency for them. Hopefully, they will get the message that consistency is how you become a successful adult."*

With this in mind, the long-term view of fatherhood naturally, then, encompasses our children's future. Said differently, the success of our children's future lies in how we raise them today. I have often said that we get a glimpse into the future through the eyes of our children. So, in this regard, humans can see into the future, we see it through our offspring. For that reason, perseverance doesn't just impact the present, it shapes the future. A father who chooses perseverance teaches his children that love is not a fleeting emotion, but a disciplined practice. A father's love and constancy become their NorthStar.

I believe this is the deeper meaning of the aforementioned and sometimes misinterpreted bible verse, Proverbs 13:22, which states that "A good man leaves an inheritance for his children's children."[7] It is widely understood that King Solomon decreed most of the Book of Proverbs and was sharing his wisdom in an effort to help future generations navigate the pitfalls of life. One can, correctly, conclude that he was aimed at helping subsequent generations find a path to prosperity. I believe that the path to prosperity also includes a legacy of good character and sound judgement.

In the end, fatherhood does not translate into unemotional, non-caring, detached stoicism. In fact, some of the most powerful moments of fatherhood emerge when a father allows himself to be vulnerable. To admit when he is wrong. To seek forgiveness. To show his children that strength includes tenderness. These deeds require tremendous courage and commitment, perhaps, more so than the quiet endurance mentioned throughout this chapter.

Through vulnerability, a father models one of life's most valuable lessons; that perseverance isn't just about holding the line, but is about creating a life with and for others that is worth living. Also, it is sometimes about shouldering the blame when things go wrong and taking less than your share of credit when things go right. Fatherhood is about trying again, sometimes with more humility, with a new understanding, and always with a deeper love.

Fatherhood, at its core, is a sacred responsibility. It demands the kind of commitment that is not flashy or loud, but steady and reliable. It is built day by day through a sticktoitiveness that stays when things get hard, that stays when there is no acknowledgment of your staying and presses on with the hope that your efforts will blossom in and throughout your children's lives.

In a world hungry for instant gratification, the persevering father becomes a radical symbol of enduring love. And in the calm strength of his commitment, he leaves behind not just memories, but a legacy woven into the very being of his children.

Bonus Theme: Prayer

In the beginning of this chapter, I mentioned that there were several additional themes that emerged from my conversations with fathers that are not listed. Perhaps the most important of the themes not mentioned, but is implied, not just throughout the book, but throughout our lives is *prayer*.

In the quiet hours before daybreak or in the stillness of night after a long day, many fathers bow their heads, not in defeat, but in devotion. Prayer, for many fathers, is not just a ritual of religious obligation, it is a lifeline, a source of strength. It is where burdens are laid down and wisdom is received. In a world that often demands more than it gives, prayer becomes a sacred space where a father finds clarity, courage, and connection.

A father's identity is often forged in the crucible of his fatherly responsibilities. He is expected to lead, protect, provide, and nurture. Yet beneath these roles lies a deeper truth, a father is also in need of guidance and direction himself. Prayer offers peace and a space where a father can be vulnerable without judgment, where he can wrestle with uncertainty and emerge with renewed purpose.

Kansas City, Missouri Entrepreneur, Pastor and Father of two adult children, W. Harris, talks about prayer as a means of strength and provision. His commentary is specifically in response to the following question, *"What are the key ingredients for strengthening a family?"*

> *"Prayer is the thing that pops up in my mind first…it has been the thing that has sustained me personally and given me strength as a father, and I believe it is the thing that has kept my family strong and together."*

Here we see Harris give credence to the power of prayer. In many respects, it affirms my belief that prayer roots a father in something greater than himself. Whether he prays to God, Allah, Yahweh, the universe, or a higher moral order, the act of prayer reminds him that he is not alone in his journey. Prayer helps a father align his actions with his principles. It becomes a mirror for self-examination and his source to continue on.

With prayer, a father does not escape his responsibilities. Prayer, instead, gives him the strength to embrace them more fully, anchored by a deep sense of who he is and what he stands for. Prayer allows a father to express fears he may not want to voice aloud. It allows him to admit when he feels inadequate, overwhelmed, or uncertain.

In a society full of distractions, prayer can be the vehicle that gets a father back to center. It can remind him to slow down, to listen, and to be fully engaged with those he loves. It can be the thing that helps him to see the error of his own ways when communication breaks down between him and other members of his household. Prayer cultivates patience, attentiveness as well as introspection. It helps a father respond rather than react to his children, not as problems to solve but as souls to nurture. And perhaps most importantly, prayer is not only for times of trouble. It can also help a father celebrate life's small as well as big blessings; a shared meal with your family on a random weeknight, a quiet evening in the safety and warmth of your home when weather conditions outside are less than ideal or the laughter of children in the house on any and every day of the week.

My dear friend, father of two young adult children and long-time Atlanta, Georgia resident, S. Lewis, talks about the joys of fatherhood and the prospect of he and his wife becoming empty nesters:

> *"One of the things that I think about now is the fact that my wife and I will soon be empty nesters…I am preparing for what my father-in-law warned me about years ago when he became an empty nester…he told me that one of the things that you'll probably notice most is how quiet the house is when your kids are gone…you will miss the sound of children being in the house."*

The significance of prayer in a father's life cannot be overstated. It is the thread that weaves through every aspect of his journey. It is not a sign of weakness, but of wisdom. Not an escape from responsibility, but a deeper embracing of it.

And very much in alignment with King Solomon's Proverb,

a father who prays leaves behind far more than material goods. He leaves an inheritance of devotion, faith, and love. His children may not remember every word he said, but they will remember the strength in his reverence to something greater than himself, in the peace in his voice when he prayed, and in the quiet moments when he bowed his head, not in defeat, but in devotion.

In the next chapter, I will discuss the origins of the troubling trope that has attempted to paint Black fathers as perpetually absent. This pesky portrayal has sought to separate African American fathers from our rightful places as heads of households and as the community leaders we are. The chapter directs our attention to the many social factors that have shaped circumstances for Black fathers. You will find that it has been societal inequities that has produced the lived experiences of African American fathers, and not their inborn values or proclivities.

CHAPTER FOUR

THE TRUTH ABOUT BLACK FATHERS

"It is a capital mistake to theorize before one has data."
Arthur Conan Doyle

There are very few things that are more powerful than an idea. Ideas have an extraordinary capacity to shape civilizations, influence behavior, and determine the course of human interaction. While some ideas like justice, equity and empathy build bridges that inspire human connection, other ideas do the opposite. One of the most enduring and destructive ideas that has ever taken root is racism—the belief that humanity can be divided, ranked, and controlled based on perceived racial differences.[1] It is more than a sentiment or a bias, it is a constructed ideology, embedded in our legal systems, cultural institutions, and interpersonal relationships. And like all powerful ideas, racism persists because it has been taught, modeled, repeated, institutionalized and has gone unchallenged in many circles.

One of the most insidious and frustrating aspects of racism is the fact that it is not born of empirical truth but is engineered by the flawed opinions of humans.[2] Pseudo-scientific theories, manipulated religious doctrine, and untrue cultural myths have all been weaponized to perpetuate it. As these narratives became widely accepted, racism embedded itself in systems that have outlived its originators.

And to boot, the ideas of racial superiority and inferiority are not scientifically grounded, though they are politically and socially potent.[3] Throughout history, those in power have manufactured racial hierarchies to justify colonization, subjugation, and segregation. By turning human differences into justifications for dominance, racism has become a tool for economic and social control. It has been used to manipulate the minds of millions of people.

In America, one of the inventions of racism has been a far less than favorable portrayal of African American men. Some argue that the African American male image has been under siege since before the inception of the country. In fact, one could claim that the phenomenon got its roots at the onset of the Trans-Atlantic Slave Trade. On the coast of West Africa and aboard the ships of slave merchants, enslavers deemed it necessary to emasculate and denigrate the male captives in an effort to discourage insurrections. The phenomenon would continue in significant ways on American soil during the country's darkest period, American chattel slavery.

Many scholars have argued that the entire Black family became the target of enslavers once in America, and with the Black male representing the head of the Black family, his persona, his very embodiment had to be weakened. After the abolition of slavery and immediately following Reconstruction, during Jim Crow—the nadir of segregation, the phenomenon reached arguably its zenith. Progressive African American males were often the target of irrational lynch mobs, determined to put these "uppity niggers" in their place.[4] Today, we continue to see explicit attempts to assassinate the Black male image. One of the most enduring assaults on African American men has been the myth of the absent, disinterested, unengaged, "deadbeat" dad.

Historical Roots of the Stereotype

The stereotype of the "deadbeat" Black dad is one of the most harmful myths in American history. Rooted in centuries of systemic racism, it assigns blame to African American men for the social ills the Black community has faced while suppressing the real drivers —the long-lasting effects of chattel slavery, discriminatory policies and practices, and media bias. Debunking this false belief requires unpacking its historical origins, examining contemporary data on the involvement of fathers, and understanding the harm it inflicts on Black families and communities.

One of the most impactful purveyors of the tarnished image of African American fathers has been the United States government. In 1965, the U.S. Department of Labor published the often-referenced document known as the *Moynihan Report on the Black Family*. The document's release, coinciding with one of the most pivotal years of the Civil Rights Movement, was written by a young politician of Irish decent named Daniel Patrick Moynihan. The paper's official title was, *The Negro Family: The Case for National Action*. At the time, Moynihan was serving as the Assistant Secretary of Labor in President Lyndon B. Johnson's administration. The report was Moynihan's attempt to encourage the federal government to adopt national policies aimed at reconstructing the African American family. In this governmentally sanctioned document, Moynihan argued that the real cause of the Black community's problems was the absent Black father. He argued that the instability of the Black community stemmed mainly from the fact that there were too many Black households being led by a matriarch; that husbands and fathers were absent from nearly half of all African American households and twenty-five percent of all African American births were "illegitimate".[5] *I will address the term "illegitimate" later in the chapter.* Quite glaringly, Moynihan's theory implied Black pathology. His hypothesis curiously overlooked the legacy of chattel slavery, the long-lasting effects of the country's discriminatory practices and the second-class treatment and political disenfranchisement that African Americans were forced to navigate.

It is not far-fetched to say that Moynihan's caricatured portrayal of Black fathers has lived on for decades in America's collective psyche, much to the country's detriment. Again, Moynihan's distorted depiction of African American fathers explicitly failed to recognize America's culpability in creating most of the Black community's adversities.

American Chattel Slavery

I intentionally use the term 'chattel' to describe America's brand of enslavement. As I'm sure you are aware, another word for the term chattel is *property*. In order to ensure that America's system of enslavement endured, enslavers deemed it necessary to transform a select group of humans — Africans — into property, and thus not human. Ultimately, I believe that their attempts to transform Africans into property, failed.

Deep down, Africans never believed that we were property, and thus not human. However, the real transformation took place within the enslavers themselves, as well as their offspring. It was the enslavers who lost a bit of their own humanity in their attempts to dehumanize Africans. Still, it has been African Americans who have been saddled with the burden of proving our humanity, even when evidence has always suggested otherwise.

Make no mistake about it, the institution of slavery was extremely brutal on the mind, body and spirit of the enslaved. It was, perhaps, much more brutal on the psychological well-being of enslaved parents. Imagine the powerlessness an enslaved father felt when a child was sold to another enslaver on a plantation miles away. The Black family was very much subject to the circumstances of White households. Debt or death in an enslaver's family could result in disruption for African American families. It was under these unspeakable circumstances that Black fathers attempted to parent their children.[6]

Moynihan's distorted depiction of the so-called absent Black father versus the Black matriarch failed to acknowledge the resilience of the Black family. His portrayal of African American fathers certainly did not take into consideration the range of their lived experiences. His interpretation definitely did not account for the volatility of an enslaved father's existence. The truth is, many enslaved fathers served as the primary caretakers for their families and communities, in spite of the conditions that enslavement wrought.[7]

We have become somewhat accustomed to the stories of

enslaved men serving as antagonists, especially in regard to them leading plantation revolts and insurrections. We are less familiar, however, with the narrative that many served as great fathers and father-figures for their families and communities. Too often, the narrative of slavery has pointed to a supposed pathology in Black people and less to the poverty, oppression and structural racism that it caused for Black people to navigate.[8]

Interrelatedly, one of slavery's legacies has been a positioning of Black masculinity in subordination to White masculinity. White men have largely been depicted in authoritative and powerful ways in and throughout our society but are allowed to be seen as boys when their behaviors result in mischief, misconduct or worse.[9] Think of 12-time Olympic medalist, Ryan Lochte, when accused of vandalizing a Rio de Janeiro gas station bathroom during the 2016 Olympic games in Brazil. Much of the commentary surrounding the fiasco was a "boys will be boys" narrative, even though Lochte was 32 years old at the time of the incident. But opposite to White men, Black men are often depicted as boys in relationship to power and authority and as men when it's convenient and especially when attempting to paint us as derelicts and criminals.[10] Think of 12-year-old Tamir Rice when playing with a toy gun in a Cleveland, Ohio park. As you may recall, when the narrative unfolded about the incident, we discovered that the police officer who shot and killed Rice, described him as a 20-year-old man with a black handgun.[11]

With regard to the institution of slavery, enslavers (White men) positioned themselves in paternalistic ways to Black men, thus suppressing Black fathers' abilities to parent their families. Slavery completely limited the ability of the enslaved to do most things, they controlled very few aspects of their lives, so raising a family was nearly impossible. Enslaved fathers were not even allowed to have their names on a child's birth certificate. The names of the mother and the enslaver were the only names permitted.[12]

The denial of Black masculinity, Black male authority and thus, Black fatherhood was central to the success of American Chattel Slavery. An enslaved father could never outwardly protect the safety of his family without, in the end, risking his own safety as well as the safety of his entire family. A defiant enslaved father could precipitate the sale of a relative to another plantation. So, enslaved fathers, as a result, took on a secondary role in the lives of their offspring. The secondary role that enslaved fathers assumed was also precipitated by the fact that many enslaved fathers lived on different plantations, away from their wives and children. Yet, many enslaved fathers managed to have considerable influence on the lives of their children, despite a system that actively undermined their authority and attempted to disempower them in every aspect of their lives.[13]

No, enslaved fathers did not have the kind of power that was acknowledged in a larger context, but that does not mean that their internal communities and families did not recognize their authority. Many were celebrated for their quiet strength and admired for their silent resistance of a system that was quite imposing and oppressive. Some were acknowledged for their quick wit in the face of irrational madness and for enduring inhumane treatment, issued by inhumane overseers.[14]

Without a shadow of doubt, the Black family suffered

greatly because of the brutal tactics of slavery. And if Black fathers were indeed absent, it was in connection to the economic, social and legal strain that slavery placed on the Black community. Unquestionably, the legacy of the Black family being led by a matriarch can be traced back to slavery. The Moynihan Report drew on this dysfunctional legacy, while overlooking the lived experiences of Black people. Once again, many enslaved fathers had an influential presence in the lives of their children, despite the weakening blow that slavery caused. Many enslaved fathers maintained a significant role as protector and provider, even if in limited ways.

In our analysis of the modern Black family, and Black fatherhood specifically, we must not look at the immediate household structure only, but instead consider the fluidity, adaptability and resilience of the entire community. Many African American families, and fathers specifically, go through great lengths to maintain a presence in lives of their children. Contemporary analyses of the family, in many regards, have been based on a Eurocentric, middle-class viewpoint, with an almost exclusive focus on co-habitation. To better understand Black families, we must refrain from normalizing the family structure on Eurocentric standards, and Black fatherhood, solely, on co-habitation. Many African American fathers maintain considerable presence and influence while living apart from their children. Much of modern family analysis and father involvement has hinged on the marital status of parents at the time of a child's birth. A father, not being married to the mother of a child, does not automatically translate into a father not being involved in a child's life.[15]

This brings me back to the term "illegitimate". I have

always taken umbrage with the term illegitimate, especially in reference to human life. I have an aversion to the term, partly, because it seems to disregard the gift of life. I also lament the term because of its connection to its most common synonym, illegal or unlawful. There is nothing illegal or unlawful about childbirth. The term illegitimate insinuates a departure from man-made law, while ignoring universal or God-given law. God gives life, with human assistance. The term, in my opinion, attempts to bestow life giving power to humans only, with no reverence for God. A child being born out of wedlock does not mean that he or she is out of the will of God. Or that his or her birth is forbidden or that the father will be out of the child's life. Many African American fathers are quite involved in their children's lives even though they are not married to their children's mother or don't physically reside with their children.

Current Data on Black Fathers

When it comes to Black fathers, we have almost always been portrayed as absent, uninvolved and disengaged, with very little to no impact on our families or communities. For decades, the image of the Black father in America has been tainted by persistent stereotypes that we are inattentive, disinterested, or uncommitted to our children. This portrayal has appeared almost everywhere; in governmental documents like the Moynihan Report to newspaper articles and cable news coverages, shaping public perceptions and opinions, and informing public policy.

Some of the more powerful depictions have taken place

via mass media broadcasts, perhaps most impactful via prime-time television programming. Excluding *Cliff Huxtable* of the 1980s sitcom *The Cosby Show*, I personally recall African American fathers being depicted as perpetually angry, absurdly clumsy, or completely absent in many 1970s, 1980s and 1990s sitcoms. Take *The Fresh Prince of Bel-Air* and even *Good Times* for example; sure, *The Fresh Prince of Bel Air* had Uncle Phil, but the whole premise of the sitcom was built around the fact that the main character was sent to live with his West Coast relatives, away from a single-mother-led household in Philadelphia. If you watched the show, I am sure that you recall the episode where his father, played by Ben Vereen, finally shows up, but vanishes at the conclusion of the episode to The Fresh Prince sobbing the words, *"how come he don't want me."*

My example of the 1970s sitcom, *Good Times*, may be throwing you off a bit because of the show's patriarch, James Evans, played by John Amos. However, those of you who are familiar with the show will recall that James Evans was killed off of the show during Season 4 of the sitcom. The show then slips into a rather typical portrayal of a struggling, fatherless Black family, being led by a matriarch.

Cable news outlets have, too, repeated the "deadbeat dad" trope even when fatherhood status is not exactly germane to the storyline; like when discussing African American men who have been murdered. You may recall that during the coverage of George Floyd's murder, some news outlets found a way to squeeze into the storyline the fact that Floyd had been, to some degree, estranged from two of his adult children.[16] Also, during coverage of Walter Scott's murder at the hand of North Charleston Police Officer, Michael Slager, we discovered that South Carolina's child support policy was the looming antagonist of the scenario. At the conclusion of the encounter, we found out that Mr. Scott was actually attempting to flee an arrest warrant for a lack of child support payments.[17] Scott was likely trying to avoid jail time, as he had recently served time on three separate occasions due to the seemingly punitive child support policy that often results in the criminalization of Black fathers.

In the end, these alarming headlines coupled with data about non-payment of child support are myopic. They ignore systemic barriers like low wages, unstable employment, and discriminatory policy enforcement that have been extremely harmful and deleterious to Black fathers, specifically, and the Black community, overarchingly. To better understand the patterns of Black father involvement, we must examine broader socio-economic conditions. Black men in the United States experience higher rates of unemployment, under-employment and incarceration compared to fathers from other ethnic groups. According to the Bureau of Justice Statistics, Black men are imprisoned at over five times the rate of White men even when convicted of similar crimes.[18] Extended incarceration stints, not only, remove fathers from their homes, but they also create persistent legal and social barriers to gainful employment, fueling a cycle of financial instability.

Also, welfare policies introduced in the 1990s, particularly the Personal Responsibility and Work Opportunity Act of 1996, attached punitive child support requirements and criminal sanctions to non-custodial parents.[19] This policy disproportionately affected Black fathers. Many fathers struggled to make court mandated payments due to incomes too meager to support basic living expenses, leading to mounting backpay penalties, legal complications, and even jail time for some. These structural obstacles, rather than a father's willingness or lack thereof, more accurately explain gaps in child support records.

Yet, beneath the surface of these daunting obstacles, and the disparaging depictions that follow, lie fruitfully successful examples of Black fatherhood that defy common stereotypes. There are a number of fathers who take great pride in being primary caregivers for their families. Some also provide care for extended family members and close relatives. In recent years, there have been a handful of studies that have highlighted this very fact. In addition to research findings that indicate that Black fathers are much more active in their children's lives than once believed, some studies have shown that African American fathers have actually led the way when compared to fathers from other ethnic backgrounds.

A 2023 study entitled, *The Myth of Low-Income Black Fathers' Absence From the Lives of Adolescents*, published by the *Journal of Family Issues*, confirmed the findings from a 2013 CDC study [20] that non-residential Black fathers, with children across all age groups and socio-economic levels, are more involved with their children than fathers from other racial and ethnic groups. Examples of involvement included activities like talking with their children several times per week. According to the study, nearly half of non-residential Black fathers (49%) reported speaking with their children several times a week, significantly more than their White (30%) and Hispanic (22%) counterparts. The article further emphasized that Black fathers of young children (ages 5 and under) are just as engaged as fathers from other racial and ethnic backgrounds. Across various socio-economic levels and living arrangements—whether co-residential or non-residential—African American fathers were found to be equally, and often more, involved in caregiving and playing with their children compared to fathers from other groups.[21]

As the title of the 2023 article suggests, the main focus of the study was aimed at the involvement or lack thereof, of low-income African American fathers, a group most associated with the myth of absenteeism. Dissimilar to former studies that focused solely on the perceptions of fathers, themselves, regarding their involvement in their children's lives, this study concentrated on the perspectives of adolescent children regarding their perceptions of closeness to and interactions with their fathers. In the end, the study corroborated the conclusions of prior studies that low-income African American fathers are, in fact, just as involved in their children's lives as fathers from different socioeconomic levels and ethnic groups. The study's researchers hypothesized that there would be a difference in the involvement of low-income non-residential fathers versus co-residential fathers. Interestingly, the findings suggest that there is no measurable difference between biological fathers who reside with their adolescent children versus biological fathers who do not reside with their children.

While the findings suggest no difference in the teenagers' perceptions of closeness to or interactions with their fathers, other studies maintain that there is a correlation between achievement levels of children with co-residential fathers versus children with non-residential fathers.[22] So, my encouragement would be for legislators and policymakers to establish programs that concentrate on financial stability as well as social mobility. There is countless evidence, both qualitative and quantitative studies alike, that contend that fathers who are gainfully employed are more likely to reside with their families.

High-Intensity Caregiving Fathers

Interestingly, there is a group of African American fathers who are practically never mentioned or even thought of when the topic of fatherhood is brought up. In a 2021 study entitled, *A Portrait of Caring Black Men*, we discover that "few differences exist between Black and [W]hite men as it pertains to how they value and fulfill their caregiving and/or parenting responsibilities". It is important to note that the study defines *High-Intensity Caregivers and/or Parents* (HICP) as "people who [have] ever provided care to an adult family member or a friend who has or has had a serious illness or disability AND/OR parents who have ever cared for a child under 18 with a medical or behavioral condition or disability (i.e. special need)".[23]

The study revealed that 86% of Black men serving as High-Intensity Caregivers (HICPs) have supported adults with instrumental activities of daily living—tasks that require coordination but no physical contact. Nearly 65% have provided direct, hands-on care involving basic physical activities. Notably, Black male HICPs are more likely than their White counterparts to perform medical or nursing tasks that require specialized skills and physical involvement. When asked about the challenges of balancing work and caregiving, Black male HICPs more often point to job demands rather than family responsibilities as the primary obstacle. Over half believe that the inability to afford time off is a major reason why men hesitate to take leave for caregiving responsibilities.

Despite these differences, Black and White male HICPs share striking similarities in how they value caregiving, how they fulfill their caregiving roles, and how they perceive barriers such as limited access to paid leave. Only about half of men in both groups report having access to paid time off. And when it comes to nurturing and providing care, the gap narrows. Both Black and White fathers express deep commitment. However, the study found that Black fathers are more likely to say it is very important to feed, dress, and care for young children themselves.

Interestingly, both groups face significant barriers to caregiving. While similar percentages of Black and White fathers used savings to cover the costs of taking leave, whether paid or unpaid, Black fathers were twice as likely (30% vs. 15%) to dip into savings specifically earmarked for health needs to fund their time away from work.

As emphasized throughout this chapter, systemic racism is the central force behind the barriers that hinder many Black fathers from fully engaging in caregiving responsibilities. To promote equitable fatherhood journeys, we must implement robust policies that confront racial disparities embedded in social, economic, and legal systems—structures that disproportionately disadvantage Black men and limit their ability to care for their families.

These barriers are not isolated, they are woven into and across intersecting systems. Black fathers with caregiving responsibilities often face a labor market that pushes them into low wage jobs and exposes them to higher risks of underemployment or unemployment completely. Without fair access to well-paying jobs, Black men, more so than White men, struggle to build savings and disposable income, both of which are essential for managing caregiving costs.[24]

The challenge is even greater for Black fathers entangled in the criminal legal system. Discriminatory policies and practices, such as over-policing, mandatory minimums, courtroom biases, and the high cost of legal fees, have led to the disproportionate incarceration of Black men. Their separation from family not only disrupts physical access to their children, but also compounds caregiving barriers, especially for those with child support obligations prior to incarceration.

In the end, believing in the "absent Black father" stereotype inflicts real harm on the Black family, the Black community, and on public policies that affect the country overarchingly. It also stigmatizes Black mothers, casting them as sole providers, void of love and support from their men. It justifies punitive policies like the aforementioned harsh child support laws, welfare restrictions and criminalizes low income, rather than investing in job creation and social programs that lead to gainful employment. Belief in the stereotype continues to undermine Black fathers' self-worth by equating their worth with bureaucratic rules instead of real relationships. It, as well, runs the risk of shaping the self-perception of Black children, who may internalize the belief that "good fathers" are inherently White and middle-class.

By continuing to perpetuate this false narrative, society

misses the opportunity to address its root causes. We must contextualize Black fatherhood with broader discussions that include an acknowledgement of poverty, under-employment, unemployment, and inequality. We must champion fatherhood support across all socio-economic levels and nurture the strengths that already exist in our communities.

A reframing of the real story of Black fatherhood means amplifying the real truth and not a myth. We do this by highlighting positive father-child relationships and interactions. Portray Black fathers as the multifaceted individuals that we are—educators, lawyers, engineers, electricians, coaches, counselors, carpenters, scientists, doctors, entrepreneurs, and activists—who balance responsibilities at home and in our communities. Reform public policy to focus on collaboration rather than punishment. Invest in job placement, fair wage initiatives, and workforce development in underserved neighborhoods. Fund community programs and fatherhood initiatives that encourage mentorship, parenting skills, and peer support. Legislators and civic leaders must advocate for curriculum and educational material that explore the real history of the Black family in America, showing how resilience and solidarity have always been at its core.

The myth of the "absent Black father" is neither benign nor inevitable. It grew from centuries of racial oppression and has been shaped by a collective, yet selective narrative. It has been sensationalized by biased media coverage and perpetuated by policies that punish rather than empower. The truth is, a more accurate narrative already exists, one of Black fathers who love passionately, lead wisely, and fight daily, against structural racism and other inequities in an effort to provide for our families. Telling that truer story requires a commitment to listen to our lived experiences, to scrutinize societal assumptions, and to reshape public discourse so that it honors truth over trope. When we do this, we not only honor Black fathers and families, but we also strengthen the professed foundations of a just America.

Special Note:

> *Throughout this chapter, I made references to a 1965 governmentally sanctioned document written by the, then, Assistant Secretary of Labor, Daniel Patrick Moynihan. You may have noticed that I took special care to emphasize his Irish heritage. Here's why. When Irish immigrants arrived during the 18th and 19th centuries, especially during and after the Great Famine, they were running away from a caste system of oppression and poverty in Europe. On American soil, their conditions were often compared to that of enslaved Africans. In urban cities, Irish immigrants and free African Americans were often thrown together in the same neighborhoods/ghettos, working side by side on railroads, shipping docks, and domestic labor jobs.*[25] *Cultural mingling was common between the two groups as well. They socialized, intermarried, and developed a shared culture of survival in the face of discrimination. Both groups were marginalized and caricatured in early American media coverage, the Irish often portrayed as foolish and African American portrayed as criminal. In many cases, they fought together against discrimination, police brutality and economic exclusion.*
>
> *However, as Irish immigrants began to assimilate into*

White American culture, many began to distance themselves from African Americans in order to gain social and economic acceptance. This even included opposing abolitionist efforts and aligning with White supremacist ideologies to secure jobs and political power. As my good friend and fellow scholar, Dr. Louis Woods, would say, the Irish had to join the "Whiteness Gang."[26]

This is an important point to make, as Moynihan's ancestors were once in a similar position as African Americans. Some scholars argue that if it were not for the assistance of African Americans, Irish immigrants would not have survived the early days of their arrival. So, in many respects, his stance against African Americans could be classified as traitorous or in the least hypocritical, and definitely myopic.

Here's my question/point: Why would he take such a position when he and his people had already fully assimilated into White American society? There was no need to continue to leverage the power of the United States Government against Black folk. But racism and its concomitant irrationality is and has always been baffling.

CHAPTER FIVE

CONCLUSION

"It is not good for the man to be alone; I shall make him [an ezer kenegdo]."
Genesis 2:18 (Hebrew Bible)

According to several biblical scholars, the phrase *ezer kenegdo*, in the Hebrew bible, translates into *warrior, strong help,* or *man's perfect match*. The phrase was used when describing the creation of Eve in relationship to Adam. In fact, the word *Ezer* was used twenty additional times throughout the Old Testament to describe God himself.[1]

Up to this point, I have concentrated exclusively on Black Fatherhood as this book is, of course, dedicated to the accomplishments of Black fathers. However, I would be foolishly myopic if I did not mention the unbridled brilliance of Black mothers, and Black women in general. Not only are they the most educated and accomplished demographic in our country, they have also been, arguably, the most devoted to the overall success of the Black family.[2]

In prior publications, I have challenged the question of the Black male's so-called extinction in America. I have concluded that our extinction is improbable, largely, because the human spirit is extremely persistent and simply will not die off that easily. I have also come to this conclusion because the Black community, collectively, has fought through centuries of oppression, and has survived treacherously harmful conditions.

If the Middle Passage couldn't exterminate us, and American Chattel Slavery followed by Jim Crow couldn't defeat us, then surely the circumstances of today cannot eliminate us.

However, I have ultimately concluded that our—the Black Male's—extinction is not possible because of the unconquerable souls of an extremely dedicated group of supporters, our women. The Black man has the Black woman at his side, and she is fiercely tenacious about the protection of her family. She is the epitome of the "Mama Bear". She fights not just for her cubs, but for her entire family.

This notion that the Black male is on the brink of extinction has circulated in both academic and cultural circles for decades.[3] It, too, is a narrative rooted in systemic oppression and media distortion. This theory, however, collapses under the weight of a deeper truth, the Black man is not alone. His survival, his flourishing is tethered to a force both ancient and immediate, both tender and ferocious. That force is the Black woman. Her presence is not just supportive, it is foundational. She is the shield, the strategist, the nurturer, and the warrior. Her love is not passive, it is quite active. And because of her, extinction is not only improbable, it is impossible.

The Black woman's role in the survival of the Black man is not a recent development, it is a historical constancy. From the plantation to the protest line, from the pulpit to the policy room, she has stood as a guardian of his legacy. Her tenacity is not born of convenience but of necessity. She has had to fight for her children, her partner, and herself in a society that often seeks to erase them all. The "Mama Bear" metaphor is fitting, but it only scratches the surface. She has also been the organizer of resistance. She was the backbone of the civil rights movement, making sure that the Black family could withstand the storms of poverty, racism and violence.

Consider the countless mothers who have turned grief into activism, who have transformed mourning into movements. Their cries have echoed through communities and courtrooms, demanding justice not just for their sons but for all sons as well as daughters. The Black woman's love is not just sentimental, it is tactical. It is the kind of love that builds institutions, that educates generations, that reclaims narratives.

The Black man, and thus the Black father's identity is not formed in isolation. It is shaped by our children, our community, our history, and most intimately, our women. She affirms my humanity when the world tries to deny it. She sees my potential when society doubts it. She reminds me of my worth when misguided statistics attempt to reduce me to a number. In her eyes, I am not a threat nor a burden. I am her partner. I am a father to her children. I am her king.

The Black man and woman are forever linked. Our interdependence is our strength. It is the kind of strength that defies division. In a society that attempts to put Black men and women in opposition to each other, our unity can be both inspiring and revolutionary. It becomes a kind of rebellion against division. It stands as a bold declaration of mutual love and respect.

Again, one of the most damaging societal myths is that of the "absent Black father". It is a narrative that ignores data, dismisses truth, and erases the lived reality of millions of people. And just as insidious is the myth that Black women are the mere victims of this absence. In truth, they are the ones who have held the family down. They have filled gaps, not with resentment, but with resolve. They have raised sons to be men of integrity, and daughters to be women of virtue.

And when Black fathers are present, as we often are, it is the Black mother who amplifies our presence. She celebrates our victories, shields our vulnerabilities, reinforces our authority, and challenges our stagnation. She is not a passive observer of our journey, she is the co-author of our story.

Again, the extinction of the Black male is not possible, not because the strongholds of oppression have weakened, but because the power of love has strengthened. The Black woman's love is not just emotional, it is celestial. It is a force that disrupts destruction and demands recognition. It is a love that builds both families and futures.

To honor the Black man, we must honor the Black woman. To acknowledge her presence is to secure our legacy. And the recognition of our bond is to understand that extinction is not our destiny, victory is.

A Better America

If truth be told, America would not be the country that it is today, if it were not for Black fathers. America is a great place, but I believe it would be an even better place if public discourse told the truth about us and if public policies were truly aimed at fair and equitable outcomes. Fair and equitable policies would lead to transformation that would ripple across every layer of our society. Unbiased treatment could and would dismantle systemic barriers that often separate Black fathers from our families. Children would grow up with stronger models of leadership and love, helping to reshape long-standing misunderstandings and misnomers. Equitable support would allow Black fathers to invest more deeply in our communities, our neighborhoods and other local institutions.

Removing hiring biases and wage disparities would unlock the full potential of America's economy. Fair access to healthier networks and increased capital would fuel business creation as well as innovation in all communities, creating exponential growth in historically underserved communities. With a more economically equitable country, Black fathers could more effectively build and pass down wealth, breaking cycles of generational poverty.

Acknowledging the truth about Black fatherhood would dismantle archaic stereotypes and enrich the national story with examples of love, sacrifice, and perseverance. The telling of a truer story would lead to better educational outcomes for Black children who are supported by fathers who are empowered to advocate and engage. Reducing systemic stressors would improve mental health outcomes, allowing Black men to thrive emotionally and spiritually. The Black man, assessed accurately, could in the end, lead to a restoration of our trust in American institutions like law enforcement, the criminal legal industry, and the educational system, making them more just and accountable.

When Black fathers are properly supported, unity is fostered, empathy is enhanced, and shared responsibility across racial lines increase. America would truly move closer to its ideals of liberty and justice for all, led by the example of men who have long embodied strength and grace under pressure. Imagine a nation where the truth about Black fatherhood is not just acknowledged but celebrated. That America would be more whole, more just, and more powerful.

America stands at a moral and cultural crossroads. For centuries, the nation has grappled with its promise of liberty and justice for all, while systematically denying those very ideals to the Black community, and Black men specifically. These men, often portrayed through distorted lenses, have endured exclusion, criminalization, and erasure. Yet we have persisted, quietly and powerfully shaping families, communities, and the moral fabric of this nation. The question is not whether Black fathers matter, but how much stronger America would be if we were treated with fairness and dignity. The answer may lead to a kind of national renewal, one rooted in truth, justice, and the restoration of a vital part of American life.

At the heart of every thriving society is the family. And Black fathers, when supported and treated equitably, serve as anchors of strength and stability for many of those families. Contrary to the harmful myths, studies have consistently shown that Black fathers are among the most involved in our children's lives, even when facing systemic forces like mass incarceration, economic disenfranchisement, and biased child welfare policies, which attempt to sever our presence.

Imagine an America where these barriers are done away with. Where Black men are not disproportionately targeted by the criminal legal system, but instead empowered to lead, nurture, and protect. Families would flourish. America would flourish. Children would grow up with models of resilience and responsibility. Communities would be strengthened by the visible, active presence of fathers who are no longer forced to fight for our legitimacy. The ripple effect would be profound; lower crime rates, improved educational outcomes, and a renewed sense of belonging.

Fair treatment of the Black family is not just a moral imperative; it is an economic one. Discrimination has long hindered the economic potential of the Black family, and thus the American family as a whole. These barriers harm individual families and rob the nation of innovation and productivity. In an equitable America, Black men would be fully included in the workforce, not just as laborers but as leaders, creators, and visionaries. We would have access to the tools needed to build businesses, invest in our communities, and pass down prosperity. The economic impact would be staggering, billions in lost productivity reclaimed, new industries born, and generational poverty broken. America would not just be richer in dollars, it would be richer in dignity and esteem.

As I have said repeatedly, the story of Black fatherhood has been distorted for far too long. Popular media often paints Black men as absent, irresponsible, or dangerous, ignoring the countless fathers who sacrifice daily, love passionately, and lead attentively. These false narratives do more than disinform, they dehumanize. A better America would tell the truth. It would honor the legacy of Black fathers who have guided our families through adversity, who have stood as moral compasses in a world that often denies our humanity. Schools would teach our stories. Films would celebrate our strength. Public discourse would shift from stereotype to sincerity. This cultural reckoning would not only uplift Black men, it would enhance the nation's identity, offering a fuller, more honest portrait of America.

The fair treatment of Black fathers is a test of America's integrity. It demands that American institutions, police departments, court rooms, and classrooms, be held accountable to the ideals they profess. It requires that laws be applied fairly, that dignity be protected, and that humanity be recognized. When humanity is recognized, communities become safer, not through surveillance, but through ownership. Children grow up believing in the promise of democracy because they see it reflected in their communities. The nation becomes more cohesive and more united, not by ignoring its past, but by confronting it and choosing a better path forward.

In the end, the fair treatment of the Black father is not about charity, it is about justice. It is to recognize that our leadership, love and labor have always been essential to America's progress. It is to build a nation where every child sees their father honored, where every man is free to lead without fear, and where truth replaces myth. This vision is not utopian, it is achievable. It begins with policy, but it must be sustained by culture, community, and courage. It calls on all Americans to reject the lies that have divided us and to embrace the truth that can unite us. Because when Black fathers rise, America rises too.

The measure of a nation is not found in its wealth or power, but in how it treats those who have been most marginalized. Black men and Black fathers have shouldered the weight of injustice with strength and grace. To honor us with fairness is to honor the best of what America can be. It is to build a future where our presence is recognized, and leadership is cultivated. That future is not only possible, but necessary. And it begins with the simple, seemingly radical act of treating Black fathers as we truly are, essential, powerful, and worthy.

Made of Steel

At the start of this book, I attempted to draw parallelisms between my dad's years of making steel while working at the steel mill in my hometown and how, as a result of his mentorship and guidance, we (his children) have become really strong and productive people, like steel. The process of steelmaking required precise timing, knowing exactly when to add each element, when to increase the heat, and when to cool them. My father seemed to have an intuitive understanding of this timing in human development. He knew when we needed guidance and when we needed space to grow on our own. Like a skilled metallurgist, he could read the signs of our development and adjust his approach accordingly.

In many respects, the tangible and metaphorical aspects of steelmaking continues to shape our lives as a result of my dad's ubiquitous presence, even today. Like the carefully controlled process of creating steel, my father's advice is always logical and impactful. His guidance has resulted in our strength. Like in steel or in character, our development comes from a balance of elements, molded attentively and shaped with compassion.

In the steel mill, my father witnessed daily how raw materials were transformed into one of the most durable man-made substances through precise processes and procedures, each step crucial to the integrity of the final product. Similarly, he approached parenting and mentorship with the same attention to detail and understanding of the process. He knew when to apply pressure, when to ease up, and most importantly, when to add the essential elements, iron and carbon (i.e. love and attention) that would make us stronger versions of ourselves.

Unfortunately, the steel mill where my father worked is in the process of being demolished. Demolition started a few months ago.[4] Though it had gone through a number of ownership changes and a few temporary shutdowns prior to its permanent closure, in many respects, the grounds where the mill use to sit will always stands as a testament to Georgetown's evolution from its rice cultivating past through its industrial period and now, perhaps, to a sleepy waterfront town, where people go to experience a bit of South Carolina's Lowcountry.

Just as the enslaved Africans brought their expertise in rice cultivation, completely transforming the region's economy, my father's commitment to fatherhood represented a new kind of expertise, one that continues on in all those he has fathered, and perhaps most significantly in those of us who are now fathers ourselves. Like the carbon that strengthens iron, his presence then and now continues to strengthen us. His presence is arguably more important today, as his current guidance helps us as we manage the ups and downs of fatherhood.

Again, what makes steel remarkable is not just its strength, but its versatility, its ability to be both firm and flexible when needed. When we were kids, my dad embodied these qualities. And as mentioned above, he still embodies these qualities. He maintains unwavering principles while showing remarkable adaptability in the face of change. Whether dealing with technological advances like the smart phone or making sure that he and my mom have WIFI coverage in their home, or adapting to current social dynamics in our community, he continues to demonstrate that true strength lies not in being resistant to change, but in the ability to bend without breaking.

In a previous chapter, you will recall that I introduced a number of my personal friends and acquaintances. In that chapter, I highlighted the various conversations that we had regarding their, and my own, overarching philosophy of fatherhood. As you may recall, one of the questions asked, *"What traditions did your father pass on to you that you've now passed to your children?"*. The question is aimed at the concept of legacy. It intends to capture the metaphysical yet meaningful heirlooms that have been passed on in their families.

Perhaps the most significant heirloom that my dad has passed on to me is the profound understanding that fatherhood is, arguably, the most important "hood" that I will ever live in. That being a father is equally as important as being a husband. And like marriage, fatherhood is a lifelong commitment that requires your undivided devotion, in perpetuity. Fatherhood is the realization that from the first moments of holding your newborn baby to when they trot off to college, and even after, your presence matters in ways that words can't fully capture.

What makes this commitment extraordinary is that it transcends physical presence. Even when fathers can't be in the same room or zip code with their children, their influence, if rooted in love and intentionality, becomes both omnipotent and omnipresent. A father's love and guidance echoes through his children's decisions, setbacks, and victories. Like one of the core principles of architecture, a father's example becomes the ground floor; the foundation to his children's belief in themselves.

Another heirloom that my father has passed on is understanding that fatherhood changes over time. The father as protector will become father as coach, no longer your children's sage in the middle of their proverbial stage, but their guide on the side. And understanding that your role as coach will, too, change to counselor. In this phase of fathering, you will advise, and they will decide. But through it all, never losing the understanding that your commitment never fades, it simply transforms.

Yet another heirloom that my father has passed on to me is kindness, not only kindness toward my children, but kindness toward others. My dad has always said that "it doesn't hurt you to be kind to others." Kindness makes the world a better place. I realize that this sounds a bit basic and perhaps pollyannaish. I'm quite sure that you've heard this principle throughout your entire life. But I think it is worth repeating as well as remembering.

I would argue that kindness is the foundation of civilization. I once read a story about a world-renowned anthropologist, when responding to a student's question about the first signs civilization, proposed that the first sign of civilization was a healed femur (a thighbone). The anthropologist went on to say that a broken leg in ancient times typically translated into certain death. She offered the logic that an individual with a broken leg couldn't run from danger, couldn't get to a river to drink water or couldn't hunt for food. A healed femur meant that someone stayed with a wounded colleague; that they treated the wound and helped the person get to safety and tended to that person through recovery. She reasoned that civilization started when someone helped someone else through a difficult situation.

As I write these words, our country is yet again in the throes of a kind of self-discovery. At the core of this discovery is the absence of a sense of kindness. And I'm not simply talking about a whimsical kind of kindness. Kindness to me includes fighting for other human beings, even if he or she originates from another country. Kindness means that he or she is owed "due process of the law" even if the end culminates in deportation or repatriation. I am not a lawyer, but I have come to understand that "a person must be given notice, [given] the opportunity to be heard, and then a decision be made by a neutral decision-maker." Our constitution says so.[5]

As you can see, the heirlooms of fatherhood reach beyond the material world and extend into the soul. These heirlooms are invisible yet are enduring gifts. They are possessions of principle. They result in a wealth of wisdom. They shape identities as well as choices and echo across decades, perhaps generations.

A father's sense of right and wrong becomes a child's internal compass. Even when he quietly inspires action in the community, a father's sense of integrity teaches his offspring how to stand firm in truth. These heirlooms help children navigate the complexities of life with clarity. Even the way a father endures hardships becomes a blueprint for surviving the storms of life. His quiet strength in adversity teaches that struggle is indeed a part of life. This gift equips children to stand strong, even when circumstances are the opposite of ideal.

A father's metaphysical heirlooms can affirm who his children are and where they come from. They root them in legacy, culture, and purpose. They give children the courage to fully be themselves. As well, a father's prayer life and reverence for God passes on a legacy of faith. It teaches that strength is not only physical, but spiritual too. It can become a child's source of peace, direction and hope.

A father's words of affirmation and even the life lessons he teaches through stories about his own life, shape how children see themselves and how they see the world around them. They often reveal themselves in a child's sense of liberation and expression and relay the message that their voice is their power. It helps children articulate their truth with confidence and inspires them to reach beyond limits and believe in what can be.

These heirlooms are not stored away in lockboxes, but are etched in our memories, in our character, and in our souls. They are our invisible inheritance that outlasts time, shaping not just who we become, but how we live our lives. They are also how we raise our children when we become fathers. As I've insinuated throughout this book and have said throughout my life, "our children will be who they see."

Though I'm blessed to still have my dad here on earth with me, he has already left a wonderful legacy. He has been the epitome of fatherhood. And not just for me and my brother, but in many respects, for the entire community of Georgetown,

South Carolina. And just like each batch of steel that came out of the now shuttered doors of the steel mill, we all carry the imprint of our making. The values and wisdom that my father imparted continue to shape not only his children, but I believe will ripple through subsequent generations, carrying a legacy as durable as the steel he helped to produce.

Looking at Georgetown today, one can still see its layers of history. From the rice fields to the steel mill, each era building on the last, each generation adding its own elements to strengthen the community. My father's contribution to this legacy, both through his work in the mill and his influence on the people around him, represents a significant layer in our town's rich history. In my book, he is indeed "A Man Made of Steel!"

CHAPTER SIX

WHAT SHOULD WE (YOU) DO NEXT?

"I am no longer accepting the things I cannot change. I am changing the things I cannot accept."
Angela Davis

This book should not end on the last page. It is not meant to. If anything, I hope this book is received as a request, an open invitation to readers to step into the work of strengthening families, honoring fathers, and preserving the truth that has shaped who we have been, who we are now and who we will be in the future. The question is not simply *what did you read*, but *what will you do now that you have read it?*

Here are a few suggestions that you might focus your energy, influence, and attention:

Support Black Fathers Through Policy and Advocacy

The systems that shape fatherhood (i.e. child support, custody, employment, housing, healthcare, etc.) don't change on their own. Readers can:

- Join or support organizations advocating for equitable family policies.
- Attend local hearings or community forums where fatherhood and family issues are being discussed.

- Use your voice to challenge narratives that criminalize or marginalize Black fathers.

Policies are not abstract. They are personal. They determine whether fathers can show up fully for their children or not.

Mentor the Next Generation

Every child deserves someone who sees them, guides them, and believes in their possibilities. Readers can:

- Volunteer with mentorship programs.
- Offer time, skills, or lived experience to youth organizations.
- Become a consistent presence in a young person's life.

Mentorship is legacy in motion. [1]

Build Community, Not Just Connections

Strong families grow in strong communities. Readers can:

- Support local fatherhood groups, barbershops, churches, and community centers.
- Create spaces where men can gather without judgment.
- Invest in programs that strengthen mental health, financial literacy, and emotional resilience.

Community is the soil where fathers and families root themselves.

Change the Narrative, Loudly and Publicly

The story of Black fatherhood has been distorted for generations. Change and influence the narrative. Readers can:

- Share stories that reflect truth, complexity, and humanity.
- Challenge stereotypes in conversations, classrooms, and public spaces.
- Amplify media, art, and research that honor Black fathers.

Narrative change is not cosmetic, it is cultural repair. And it requires your input.

Become the Family Griot: Archive, Preserve, and Pass It On

Every family has a keeper of memory. Readers can:

- Record elders' stories before they are lost.
- Digitize photos, letters, and home videos.
- Create family trees, oral histories, or legacy books.
- Teach children where they come from and who they come from.

When we preserve our stories, we protect our lineage from erasure.

This book is a testament to fathers who stayed, fathers who tried, fathers who struggled, and fathers who loved in ways the world hasn't always seen. But its purpose is bigger than remembrance. It is a call to action. If something in these pages inspired you, challenged you, or reminded you of your own story, then let that feeling guide your next steps. Remember, legacy is not built in grand gestures, it is built in the daily choices we make to show up for our children and for each other. The next chapter isn't written by me only. It is written by all of us. Asè.

ACKNOWLEDGEMENTS

First and foremost, I would like to thank God. For it is God who has endowed me with the mental and physical capacity to have written this book. I thank You God for my life, for the breath in my lungs, for the faculty of my mind and for the use of my body. You are my sustainer, my supplier and my savior. You have ordered my steps throughout my life, for which, I am grateful. I thank You for answered prayers, and for those that felt unanswered, but were in reality answered. Thank You for the call upon my life and for the trials and triumphs I have experienced as a result of that calling. Words fall short in expressing my love and gratitude for Your presence in my life. I am Your son and You are, indeed, my Father. Asè.

I am also incredibly thankful to a lot of people who have made this book possible. First, is my wife, Stephenie K. Smith. Our love is certain. In fact, I could not have written this book without you, because I would not have been a father without you. And, thus, to my children, Phoenix, Jordan (departed) and Chi, you all have made me a father. Thank you for that wonderful gift.

It goes without saying that I am eternally grateful for my father, Zeddie C. Smith. You are the prototype of what a father should be. Thank you for being my example. To my mother, Lillian M. Smith. Thank you for giving me life. Thank you for giving me my love of books and of the written word. Thank you, most of all, for being my prayer warrior. I know, without a shadow of doubt, that it has been your prayers that have sustained my life. And to my brother, Eric C. Smith. Our bond is unbreakable. I love you. And to my cousins/sisters, Kim and Libby, I love y'all, real bad.

To the fathers who contributed directly and indirectly to this book, I am forever grateful. There is, however, a special group whom I would like to thank, specifically. Brother Gerald "Qrunch" Bryant, Sr., Brother Tyrone "Big Ty" Taylor, Brother Anthony "A-Dub" Wilson, Brother Steve "80" Kee, Brother Vincent "82" Kee, Brother DiMond "96" Piggie, Brother Rodney "Rraah Tee" Thomas, Brother Eugene "Geno" Brown, Brother Bryant "Bernie MaQ" Jackson, Sr., Brother Cedrick "Ced the 3ntertainer" Owens, Sr., Brother Maurice "Bruhman" Oatis, Brother Jamar "17" Madge, Brother Sal "Short Cut" Madge, Brother Marvin "90" Jones, Brother Isaiah "Top" Faulkner, Brother Franko "One" Witherspoon, Brother Gerald "GB" Brown, Brother Colby "Tre Dog" Broadnax, Brother Sonny "HOF" Williams, Brother Okwar "OJ" Jale and Brother Leonard "Big Len" Searcy. Our Wednesday Night Fellowship/ Therapy Sessions inspired this book. Our conversations are not just life-changing, they are life-giving!

There's another group of gentlemen whose friendship and example of fatherhood have contributed to this book, but more importantly, have contributed to my life: Brother Montonio "Doughboy" Reid, Brother Jerome "Smiley" Johnson, Brother Carl "Willie Lump Lump" Weaver, Brother Gerald "G-Que" Eaton, Brother Ty-re "Scarface" Dixon, Sr., Brother Carl "Yard Dog" Lynch, Brother John "Big Mac" Simmons, and Brother

Stanley "FreaQy Tail" Lewis. Your friendship means the world to me. I feel off balance when I'm away from y'all for too long.

The following fathers contributed directly, as well as indirectly, to this book. Among them are lifelong friends, mentors, mentees, relatives, fraternity brothers, and gentlemen I have met at various stages of my life. They are Gregory L. Nesbit, Woodrow Nesbit, Jr, Woodrow Nesbit, Sr., Alfonzo Allen, Bernard "Spacey" Wilson, Joe Lee White, Kevin White, PaPa Joe White, Ullyses Wright, Michael McConnell, William Harris, Wrenchel Stokes, Tranis Parker, David Doiley, Everett Freeman, Jr., Greg Williams, Brother Kenny Ellison, Brother Jesse Junius, Brother Rahmaan Burns, Cedric Thomason, Terrell Jolley, Samuel Jolley, Myron McCant, Gary Jones, Dr. Vernon Howard, Jamal Davis, Anthony "AJ" Jones, Aaron Foreman, Brother Anthony "AC" Cole, Adam Rush, Brother Adam Williams, AJ Byrd, Alphonso Parson, Brother Andre Anderson, Brother Andre Butler, Brother Anthony "Amp" Burgess, Brother Anthony Willis, Brother Diandrai Webb, Antwan Daniels, Archie Wesley, Brother Ather "Doc" Keys, Jr. (Departed), Uncle Arthur Smith (Departed), Austin LeBlanc, Roman LeBlanc, B.J. Stabler, Barry Sims, Brother Ben Northington, Brother Bertram Lawson, Bernard Bessellieu (Departed), Marion Bessellieu (Departed), Jimmy "Big Jim" Dozier, Anthony "Cool Cat" Dozier, Jeffery "Big Jeff" Greene, Brandon Edington, Brandon Martin, Branden Mims, Brandon Thompson, Bryan Jones, Bryan Benson, Lewis Smith, Brother Bryan White, Brittan Motley, Brother Yuhanna Edwards, Brother Bruce Miller, Brother Bruce Randall, Cameron Young, Carlos Weathers, Carlose Estes, Charles Foust, Chiluba Musonda, Brother Chris Dobbins, Chris Evans, Chris Shobe,

Gregory Magee, Clint Risper, Carl Evans, Sr. (Departed), Carl Evans, Jr., Murray Woodard, Dr. M. Conrad Journée, Corey Syon, Craig Moore, Daelon Cravens, Brother Dr. Damien Hodge, Damon Bell, Damon Hodges, Brother Dante Combs, Brother Darnell Reid, Darnell Smith, Larnell Smith, Brother Darrell Freeman (Departed), Darryl Answer, Darryl Duncan, David Murray, David Muhammad, David Wilson, Dr. Derriell Springfield, Dr. Aaron Ellison, Thomas Amous, Leland Brooks, Derrick Smith, Dwayne Jackson, Dwayne Lewis, E.B. Wiltz, Brother Earl Green, Jr., Ed Green, Brother Eddie Vail, Brother Todd Wilcher, Brother Eric Bieniemy, Eric Boyd, Erik Dickinson, Brother Eric Evans, Eric Thompson, Eric Williams, Erik Stafford, Emmet Pierson, Wesley Fields, Tim Chatman, Brother Jason Vaughn, Fredrick McCullough, Fredrick Shaw, Brother George "GT" Thomas, Gareth Bonds, Garrett Webster, Gary Hunter, Brother Gary Jones, Jr., Gary Maltbia, Gary Stills, Brother Glenn Rice, Brother Glenn Moore, Glenn Ladson (Departed), Gregory Ashby, Brother Gregory Hayes (Departed), Henderson Hill, Jack Williams, Jackson Winsett, James Brown, Jayson Brown, James Scott, Jamie Grayson, Brother Jason Gibson, Jason Parson, Brother Dr. Jeffrey "Tré-9-Tré" Handy, Jeff Primos, Brother Jerry Davis, Jesse Hightower, Jimmy Henry, Brother Joe Hampton, Joe Harland, Brother Joe Nelson, Brother John Randle, Jonathan Truesdale, Merrell Bennekin, Joseph Macklin, Brother Dr. Josiah Sampson, Juan Nunez, Judge Jon Gray, Junior Flynn, Justin Blackburn, Corey Shepherd, Brother Kaggia Scott, Karlos Parker, Chris Parker, Sr., Chris Parker, Jr., Dantez Parker, Karriem Ali, Brother Keelronn Hatley, Keith Harris, Keith Smith, Keith Mason, Brother Kelan Mitchell, Brother Kenny "Ghetto Boy" Pierce, Paul Pierce, Sr., Paul Pierce, Jr., Brother Kenneth Moore,

Brother Kermit Ervin, Kevin "Church" Johson, Brother Dr. Kevin "Pee Wee" Williams, Dr. Kevin Armstrong, Brother Kevin "KB" Battle, Dr. Kevin McDonald, Kevin Smith, Harold Kinley, LaDale Benson, Lamar Humes, Alanzo McIntosh, Leo McIntosh, Sr. (Departed), Leo McIntosh, Jr, Michael McIntosh, Steve McIntosh (Departed), Troy McIntosh, Jason Sims, Bishop Ervin Sims (Departed), Jr., Bernard Keith, Darrin Wilson, Brother Benjamin Crump, Congressman Emanuel Cleaver II, Bob Kendrick, Mayor Quinton Lucas, Larry Gray, Brother DJ McCord, Brother LaSalle "Redneck, The Great" Chapman-Curry, Brother Lawrence "LT" Taylor, Jr., Brother Eric Austin, Brother Brian Egeston, Brother Terrance Gragg, Brother Tony Springfield, Aaron Alexander, Brother Aaron Leach, Brother LaValle White, Brother Lawerence Guinn, Leroy Smith, Lorin Crenshaw, Dr. Louis Woods, Brother Dr. Louis Ferguson, Brother Dr. Ralph Simpson, Dr. Luke Bobo, Marcus Walker, Jason Banks, Dr. Mark Bedell, Mark Jones, Brother Dr. Marques Stewart, Marquis Harris, Marvin Carolina, Jr., Marvin Daniels, Marvin Lyman, Michael Cozart, Slyvester Simmons, Herman Ford (Departed), Fredrick Ford, Otwain Ford, Tyrone Ford, Michael Ford, Robert Sparkman, Sr. (Departed), Sean Sparkman, Michael Sparkman, Melvin Huell, Sr, Melvin Huell, Jr., Mike Farris, Brother Dr. Millard Collins, Brother Dr. Miron "Shine" Billingsly, Dr. Munro Richardson, Brother Jesse Rudolph (Departed), Brother N'Gai Rudolph, Dr. Nate Thomas, Neil Johnson, Dr. Omaran Lee, Oscar Tshibanda, Dr. Oscar James, Brother Dr. Vincent Windrow, Queron Smith, Pastor Douglas Smith, Daryl Smith, Brother Dr. Rafael Harley, Randolph Walker, Reginald Johnson, Reginald Hester, Reginald Smith, Richard Butts, Aaron Butts, Sheldon Butts, Brother Rick Washington, Robbie

Faison, Brother Robert Humphrey, Brother Dr. Robert McNichols, Dr. Rob Milner, Roberto Young, Pastor Robert Davis, Rodney Adams, William Adams, Jr., William Adams, Sr., Rodney Henry, Brother Rodney Sampson, Rodney X, Dr. Roland Hemmings, Dr. Ronald Anderson, Ronald Corbin, Ron McInnis, Brother Lorin Rivers, Brother Dr. Patrick Harris, Brother Ron Miranda, Brother Scott Dixon, Ron Stigger, Brother Dr. Ronald Rochon, Ron Amos, Brother Dr. Rubin Cockrell, Brother Sam Cooper, Sean Stalling, Sean Tyler, Brother Shamann Walton, Sherman Whites, Silas Dulan, Simeon Henderson, Brother Skip Miller, Spark Bookhart, Spencer Wiggins, Gerald Morrison, Stace Morrison, Brother Stacey Franklin, Brother Stan Counts (Departed), Brother Stan Diggs, Brother Sterling Brown, Steve Barnes, Steve Hooks, Brother Steve McClellan, Brother Dr. Steven Smith, Teremy Banks, Ted Hughes, Terence "Buck" Ford, Brother Terrance Williams, Terry Riley, Thomas Balkcom, Thomas Newman, Dr. Tommy Miller, Tony Doiley, Brother Tony Muhammad, Torrence Jones, Dr. Tyrone Bates, Jr. Tyrone Aiken, Coach Tommy L. Smith (Departed), Uncle Herb Knox (Departed), Uncle James Smith, Uncle Jerry Smith (Departed), Uncle Bernie Ford, Uncle Robert "Johnny" Spratt, Uncle Otis Bullion, Uncle Alphonso Wright, Uncle James Wright, Uncle Donald Wright, Uncle Tony Wright, Uncle Algerian Wright (Departed), Uncle Calvin Wright, Uncle Walter Wright (Departed), Uncle Lonnie McConnell, Uncle Richard Bowen (Departed), Dr. Wes Parham, William Palmer, Willy Pegues, Nikki Newton, Zachary Shelton, Brother Ryan Long, Chris Madden, Leonard Stowe, Brother Leon Montgomery, Dr. Dennis Carpenter, Calvin Vick, Damian Cunningham, Brother Richard Morton, Brother Charles McKinney, Brother David

Pressley, Brother Leroy Outerbridge, Brother Talib Briscoe, Brother Kirby Davis, Brother Scott Morris, Brother Harold Cooper, Kevin Whalum, Adrian Granderson, Tyree Corley, Ernest Benson, Brother Terrell Perry, Brother Bruce Grant, Brother Ben Scott, Brother Lamont Doty, Bobby Lee, Ron Gary, Dr. Ahmed White, Damien Jackson, Brother Chris Whitmore, Sr., Brother Richard Livingston, Sammie Coe, Levi Smith, Tyrell Smith, Gerald Jenkins, Cornell Ellis, Craig McAshan, Jon Shoats, George Baldi, Glenn McKinney, Sr. (Departed), Michael Hull-Littlejohn, Bruce Williams, Brother Jared Prentiss, Corey Burton, Brother Frank Scott, Brother Trey Knox, Brother Eric Trotter, Hilbert Heyward, Brother Adam Blyden, William Green, Brother Lee Molette, Alvin Brooks, Tracey Knox, Marvin Reed, Brother Benny Gaston, Brother Jefferson Grant, Jr., Brother Mark Freeman, Louis Upkins, Brother Eric Fowler, Brother Sekou Charles, Brother Charles Lee, Jr., Ulander Giles, Reggie Thomas, Brother Antonio Howard, Maurice Goings, Quintion Williams, Brother Napoleon Harris, James-Michael Hogue, Brother Shelvy Convert, Brother Guy Johnson, Dan Smith, Lifonia Greene, Lance Conley, Dan Cranshaw, Brother Charles Wilson, Brother Harry Lee, Brother Kelly Walker, Michael West, Darrell Graham, Mr. D.J. Graham, Darrell Ward, DeVonie Cunning Kendrick, Travis Alston, Derek Alston, Orlando Britton, TL Davis, Datwon Thomas, Brother Theotis Watson, Shannon Hill, Sr., Roderick Julius, Sammy Julius, Benjamin Watkins, Sammy Watkins, Andrew Watkins, Rev. Richard Watkins, Brother Donavan Slack, Tupelo Humes, Andre Davis, George Forte, Brandon Marshall, Antonio Simmons, and Brother Calvin McMiller.

Truthfully, this is just a smattering of African American fathers that I know, personally. They are fathers who I am in contact with on a somewhat regular basis. There are thousands, if not millions more, whom I do not know, who are the antithesis to what America says about Black fathers. They are an amalgamation of fathers and father-figures who are successfully leading and loving their families across our beautiful country. They are who this book is about. I have had them on my mind as I have written this book.

A special shout out and thank you is extended to my dear friend, Derek Young. During one of our many conversations, where I was describing my father's ubiquitous presence in my life, Derek said to me, "not only was your father a steelmaker, sounds like he is made of steel." This is where the title of the book comes from. Derek is the father of four young adult children. I would not be exaggerating if I said that the topic of fatherhood comes up every single time that we've talked over our twenty-seven-year friendship. We both take great pride in being fathers.

FOREWORD

1. Steve Ivory (2007): "Universal Fatherhood: Black Men Sharing the Load". *The State of Black America 2007*: An Official Publication of the National Urban League.
2. 2 Corinthians 4: 16 – 18 (New International Version, Holy Bible): [16]*Therefore, we do not lose heart. Though outwardly, we are wasting away, yet inwardly we are being renewed day by day.* [17] *For our light and momentary troubles are achieving for us an eternal glory that far outweighs them all.* [18]*So, we fix our eyes not on what is seen, but on what is unseen, since what is seen is temporary, but what is unseen is eternal.*

INTRODUCTION

1. Jo Jones and William D. Mosher, "Fathers' Involvement with Their Children: United States, 2006-2010" *National Statistics Reports*, Number 71, Center for Disease Control, (December 20, 2013). https://www.cdc.gov/nchs/data/nhsr/nhsr071.pdf
2. Robert Monroe, "Shaping Perceptions: The Impact

of Black Fatherhood Portrayals in the Urban Media Landscape." *Medium*, (September 25, 2023). https://medium.com/raising-a-beautiful-mind/shaping-perceptions-the-impact-of-black-fatherhood-portrayals-in-the-urban-media-landscape-4b6fd8665972

3. Ibid #1

4. Tom Burell, *Brainwashed: Challenging the Myth of Black Inferiority*. (New York, NY: SmileyBooks, 2010.)

5. Dee Parmer Woodtor, *Finding a Place Called Home: A Guide to African American Genealogy and Historical Identity*. (New York, NY: Random House, 1999)

6. "Slavery on South Carolina Rice Plantations: The Migration of People and Knowledge in Early Colonial America." http://ricediversity.org/outreach/educatorscorner/documents/Carolina-Gold-Student-handout.pdf

7. Ibid #1

8. Jay Fagan, "The Myth of Low-Income Black Fathers' Absence From the Lives of Adolescents." *Journal of Family Issues*, Volume 45, Issue 1, January 10, 2023. https://journals.sagepub.com/doi/10.1177/0192513X221150987

9. Jahdziah St. Julien, "A Portrait of Caring Black Men", *New America*. February 4, 2021. https://www.newamerica.org/better-life-lab/reports/portrait-caring-black-men/

10. Jude 1:3 "Dear friends, although I was very

eager to write you about the salvation we share, I felt compelled to write and urge you to contend for the faith that was once for all entrusted to God's holy people." The New International Version Bible.

CHAPTER ONE

MY FATHER: A MAN MADE OF STEEL

1. "Slavery on South Carolina Rice Plantations: The Migration of People and Knowledge in Early Colonial America." http://ricediversity.org/outreach/educatorscorner/documents/Carolina-Gold-Student-handout.pdf

2. Making Still, https://corporate.arcelormittal.com/about/making-steel

3. Chemistry Behind Alloy Steel, https://www.leecosteel.com/news/post/how-adding-elements-changes-steel/

4. The malleability of Steel: How to Shape This Sturdy Metal, https://rowvilleengineering.com.au/the-malleability-of-steel-how-to-shape-this-sturdy-metal/#:~:text=The%20longer%20the%20steel%20stays,carbon%20and%20high%2Dcarbon%20steels (February 6, 2025).

5. Lindsey Lyles, "Thirty-Five Years Ago, the Coastal Southeast Had a White Christmas. Was It The Last?" *Garden & Gun*, https://gardenandgun.com/articles/thirty-five-years-ago-the-coastal-southeast-had-a-white-christmas-was-it-the-last/. (December 18, 2024).

6. Brook C. Feeney and Nancy L. Collins, "New Look at Social Support: A Theoretical Perspective on Thriving through Relationships." *National Institutes of Health, National Library of Medicine.* https://pmc.ncbi.nlm.nih.gov/articles/PMC5480897/#_ci93_

7. J.P. Stewart, "Griot." *EBSCO*, https://www.ebsco.com/research-starters/social-sciences-and-humanities/griot. (July 2022)

8. Michael Harriot, *Black AF History: The Un-Whitewashed Story of America.* (New York, NY, HarperCollins Books, 2023.)

9. Nilo Puglisi, Valentine Rattaz, Nicolas Favez and Herve' Tissot, "Father Involvement and emotion regulation during early childhood: a systematic review." *BMC Psychology*, 12(1):675, November 2024. https://www.researchgate.net/publication/385940929_Father_involvement_and_emotion_regulation_during_early_childhood_a_systematic_review

10. Wendy Wang, "American Dads are more involved than ever: Especially College-Educated and Married Dads." *Institute for Family Studies: Strong Families Sustainable Societies*, October 24, 2023. https://

ifstudies.org/ifs-admin/resources/briefs/ifs-wang-fatherstimebrief-oct2023-1.pdf

11. Sonja Starrick, "A Father's Vital Role in Teaching Children Empathy and Emotional Intelligence." Jai Institute for Parenting. June 16, 2023. https://www.jaiinstituteforparenting.com/a-fathers-vital-role-in-teaching-children-empathy-and-emotional-intelligence

12. Kathryn Edin, Laura Tach, and Ronald Mincy, "Claiming Fatherhood: Race and the Dynamics of Paternal Involvement among Unmarried Men." The ANNALS of the American Academy of Political and Social Science, Volume 621, Issue 1, January 1, 2009. https://journals.sagepub.com/doi/10.1177/0002716208325548

CHAPTER TWO

THE FATHERS IN MY FAMILY

1. The Town of Boley, Oklahoma. https://www.thetownofboley.org/

2. Nashville's Farmers' Market. https://www.nashvillefarmersmarket.org/

3. Exchange, Volume 22, Number 2, EAP Association. file:///C:/Users/Owner/Downloads/ExchangeV22N2.pdf

4. NRI Administration, "How Does A Relocation

Company Sell Your House?" NRI: Taking Relocation Personally. https://nrirelocation.com/relocation-company-selling-house/

5. Jahdziah St. Julien, "A Portrait of Caring Black Men", *New America*. February 4, 2021. https://www.newamerica.org/better-life-lab/reports/portrait-caring-black-men/
6. Friedrich von Schiller Quote. "It is not flesh and blood, but the heart which makes us fathers and sons." https://www.goodreads.com/quotes/461630-it-is-not-flesh-and-blood-but-heart-which-makes
7. Proverbs 13:22, "A good [man] leaves an inheritance for their children's children, but a sinner's wealth is stored up for the righteous."

CHAPTER THREE

MY FRIENDS ARE GREAT FATHERS

1. Jo Jones and William D. Mosher, "Fathers' Involvement with Their Children: United States, 2006-2010" *National Statistics Reports*, Number 71, Center for Disease Control, (December 20, 2013). https://www.cdc.gov/nchs/data/nhsr/nhsr071.pdf
2. Nilo Puglisi, Valentine Rattaz, Nicolas Favez and Herve' Tissot, "Father Involvement and emotion regulation during early childhood: a systematic review." *BMC Psychology*, 12(1):675,

November 2024. https://www.researchgate.net/publication/385940929_Father_involvement_and_emotion_regulation_during_early_childhood_a_systematic_review

3. Cooper Carry Architects. https://www.coopercarry.com/projects/opry-mills/
4. Guy Saffold, "Leading From Behind: The Shepherd's Way". *Leading God's Way*. https://saffold.com/blog/2016/12/15/leading-from-behind-the-shepherds-way/
5. Natasa Lazovic, Jelena R. Krulj, Sladana Vidosavijevic, and Emilija Markovic, "The Correlation Between Father Involvement and The Academic Achievement of Their Children: Meta-Analysis." *International Journal of Cognitive Research in Science Engineering and Education*, 10(30):53-60, November 17, 2022. https://www.researchgate.net/publication/366451902_The_Correlation_Between_Father_Involvement_and_The_Academic_Achievement_of_Their_Children_Meta-Analysis
6. Verner Brumley Mueller Parker, "The Important Role Fathers Play in Their Child's Life." *Mueller Family Law*, November 21, 2024. https://www.vernerbrumley.com/blog/2024/november/the-important-role-fathers-play-in-their-childs-/
7. Proverbs 13:22, "A good [man] leaves an inheritance for their children's children, but a sinner's wealth is stored up for the righteous."

CHAPTER FOUR

THE TRUTH ABOUT BLACK FATHERS

1. Merriam-Webster Dictionary. Definition of Racism. https://www.merriam-webster.com/dictionary/racism

2. Beverly Daniel Tatum, *Why Are All the Black Kids Sitting Together in the Cafeteria?: And Other Conversations About Race* (New York, NY: Basic Books, 2017).

3. Ibid #2

4. Michael Harriot, *Black AF History: The Un-Whitewashed Story of America.* (New York, NY, HarperCollins Books, 2023.)

5. U.S Department of Labor, "The Negro Family: The Case for National Action." https://www.dol.gov/general/aboutdol/history/webid-moynihan

6. Libra R. Hilde. *Slavery, Fatherhood, and Paternal Duty in African American Communities over the Long Nineteenth Century.* (Chapel Hill, NC: The University of North Carolina Press, 2020).

7. Ibid #6

8. Hasan Kwame Jeffries and Kenneth S. Greenberg. "Resistance Means More Than Rebellion." *Learning For Justice, Season 1: American Slavery.* https://www.learningforjustice.org/podcasts/teaching-hard-history/american-slavery/resistance-means-more-than-

rebellion

9. Mark Okuhata. Unchained Manhood: The Performance of Black Manhood During the Antebellum, Civil War, and Reconstruction Eras. (2014) *UCLA*. ProQuest ID: Retrieved from https://escholarship.org/uc/item/8zk1c6kj

10. Shasta Darlington and Steve Almasy, "Ryan Lochte charged by Brazilian authorities." CNN World, August 26, 2016. https://www.cnn.com/2016/08/25/americas/ryan-lochte-brazil

11. Brad Bennett, "Remembering Tamir Rice: Police shooting of 12-year-old playing with toy gun energized criminal justice reform efforts." *Southern Poverty Law Center*, November 20, 2020. https://www.splcenter.org/resources/stories/remembering-tamir-rice-police-shooting-12-year-old-playing-toy-gun-energized-criminal/

12. Ibid #6

13. Ibid #6

14. Ibid #8

15. Dwayne Curry, "Reclaiming the Narrative of Black Fatherhood." Robert Wood Johnson Foundation, June 16, 2021. https://www.rwjf.org/en/insights/blog/2021/06/reclaiming-the-narrative-of-black-fatherhood.html

16. KTLA 5 Digital Staff, *"Don't fight fire with fire: George Floyd's estranged children in Texas denounce violence."* Nation/World News. https://ktla.com/news/

nationworld/dont-fight-fire-with-fire-george-floyds-estranged-children-in-texas-denounce-violence/

17. Betsy Reed, "Walter Scott: uncertainty over arrest warrant for thousands owed in child support." The Guardian, April 10, 2015. https://www.theguardian.com/us-news/2015/apr/10/walter-scott-no-warrant-issued-child-support-traffic-stop

18. Derek Mueller. *Prisons Report Series*. December 2024. https://bjs.ojp.gov/preliminary-data-release-prisons-2023

19. Office of Child Support Services, "The Personal Responsibility and Work Opportunity Reconciliation Act of 1996. Policy & Guidance, November 1, 1996. https://acf.gov/css/policy-guidance/personal-responsibility-and-work-opportunity-reconciliation-act-1996

20. Jo Jones, Ph.D. and William D. Mosher, Ph.D., "Fathers' Involvement With Their Children: United States, 2006-2010." National Health Statistics Report, Number 71, December 20, 2013. https://www.cdc.gov/nchs/data/nhsr/nhsr071.pdf

21. Jay Fagan, "The Myth of Low-Income Black Fathers' Absence From the Lives of Adolescents." *Journal of Family Issues*, Volume 45, Issue 1, January 10, 2023. https://journals.sagepub.com/doi/10.1177/0192513X221150987

22. Natasa Lazovic, Jelena R. Krulj, Sladana Vidosavijevic, and Emilija Markovic, "The Correlation Between Father Involvement and The Academic Achievement

of Their Children: Meta-Analysis." *International Journal of Cognitive Research in Science Engineering and Education*, 10(30):53-60, November 17, 2022. https://www.researchgate.net/publication/366451902_The_Correlation_Between_Father_Involvement_and_The_Academic_Achievement_of_Their_Children_Meta-Analysis

23. Jahdziah St. Julien, "A Portrait of Caring Black Men", *New America*. February 4, 2021. https://www.newamerica.org/better-life-lab/reports/portrait-caring-black-men/

24. Ibid #22

25. Louis L. Woods, "Killing for Inclusion: Racial Violence and Assimilation Into the Whiteness Gang," Volume 79: Chapter 13, The Trayvon Martin in US: An American Tragedy. (New York, NY: Peter Lang Publishing, 2015).

26. Ibid # 24

CHAPTER FIVE

CONCLUSION

1. Ezer Kenegdo, https://www.zoweh.org/the-daily-orientation/events/the-deepening-weekend/ezer-kenegdo
2. Nikki Katz, "Black Women Are the Most Educated Demographic in America," ThoughtCo.com. https://www.thoughtco.com/black-women-most-educated-

group-us-4048763
3. J.T. Gibbs (1988). Young, Black, and Male in America: An Endangered Species. U.S. Department of Justice: Office of Justice Programs. NCJRS Virtual Library. https://www.ojp.gov/ncjrs/virtual-library/abstracts/young-black-and-male-america-endangered-species
4. Brian Taylor, "Demolition underway at former SC steel mill." *Recycling Today*, May 7, 2025. https://www.recyclingtoday.com/news/georgetown-steel-liberty-gfg-south-carolina-demolition-redevelopment-ip-paper/
5. Michael Tan, "What is Due Process?" ACLU News & Commentary, May 28, 2025. https://www.aclu.org/news/civil-liberties/what-is-due-process

CHAPTER SIX

WHAT SHOULD WE (YOU) DO NEXT?

1. Tony Dungy. The Mentor Leader: Secrets to Building People and Teams that Win Consistently. (Carol Stream, IL: Tyndale House Publishers, Inc., 2010).

ABOUT THE AUTHOR

Dr. Rodney D. Smith is co-founder and co-managing partner of Sophic Solutions, a Kansas City-based change management consulting firm. Smith is the firm's lead authority on issues related to diversity, equity, inclusion and belonging. His expertise specifically pertains to student achievement, with a special emphasis on African American student achievement, urban education and culturally responsive pedagogy.

He recently served as the inaugural Vice President for Access and Engagement at William Jewell College where he led all of the college's diversity, equity, inclusion and belonging initiatives. In this role, he chaired the Justice, Equity, Diversity, and Inclusion (JEDI) Team and worked with students, staff and faculty toward increasing cross-cultural engagement at all levels across the campus community. He also served as the chair for the Racial Reconciliation Commission, a group of scholars who were commissioned to investigate the College's history as a slaveholding institution.

Smith also holds a Graduate Adjunct Professorship with the School of Education at the University of Missouri-Kansas City, where he specializes in courses that address racial and ethnic diversity, and cultural understanding.

Over the course of a 30-year career, Dr. Smith's scholarly interests have taken aim at the implications of race and racism in American society.

Dr. Smith also wrote and published his first book ***Are We Really Crabs in a Barrel: The Truth and Other Insights About the African American Community*** in 2016. As well, he wrote a chapter in an anthology entitled ***The Trayvon Martin in Us: An American Tragedy*** *in 2015.*

Smith holds a Doctor of Education Degree from Tennessee State University, a Master of Education Degree, also from Tennessee State University, and a Bachelor of Arts Degree from Morris Brown College. He is married to Stephenie K. Smith, and they are the proud parents of two young adult children.

APPENDIX

INTERVIEW QUESTIONS FOR FATHERS

1. What's your philosophy on fatherhood?
2. What's your secret to building relationships with your children?
3. What are the key ingredients for strengthening a family?
4. Do you have any regrets about something you wish you would have done?
5. Which mistakes taught you the greatest life lessons?
6. When did you realize you were no longer a boy?
7. What has been your greatest struggle as a father?
8. How would you define a father's role at home?
9. What traditions did your father pass on to you that you've now passed to your children?
10. What kind of relationship do you have with your father?
11. What's the best decision you've ever made as a father?

12. What's one thing you wanted to hear your father say to you?
13. Which has been more important to you, being a father or being a husband?
14. What has been your greatest accomplishment as a father?
15. What has been your strategy in challenging your children to do more?
16. What was your vision and purpose for your children?
17. What fatherhood related situation "tested your mettle", and what did you learn about yourself by dealing (or not dealing) with it?
18. What do you remember about the birth of each of your children?
19. Were you ever scared to be a father?
20. What three words represent your approach to fatherhood?

www.ingramcontent.com/pod-product-compliance
Ingram Content Group UK Ltd.
Pitfield, Milton Keynes, MK11 3LW, UK
UKHW021523300726
14060UKWH00018B/752/J

9 780997 524147